# Dialects of American English

Revised Edition

Carroll E. Reed

The University of Massachusetts Press

Brief acknowledgment of permission to use material previously published appears at the bottom of the page containing that material; full statements for the purpose of copyright protection appear on page 99.


Library of Congress Catalog Card Number 76–45049
ISBN 0–87023–233–9
Printed in the United States of America
First Printing 1967 by The World Publishing Company
Second Printing 1973
Revised Edition 1977

# Contents

# *Acknowledgments*

To Hans Kurath and Raven McDavid I am greatly indebted for much inspiration and many favors, including their friendly co-operation in permitting me to use the files of the Linguistic Atlas of the United States. I am also grateful to Virginia McDavid, Mary Atwood, Alva Davis, Albert Marckwardt, and David Reed for their part in making the writing of this little book possible.

Special credit is due the American Council of Learned Societies, sponsors and publishers of the Linguistic Atlas of the United States, as well as to the University of Michigan Press for permission to use maps and data from Hans Kurath's *Word Geography of the Eastern United States* (Ann Arbor: University of Michigan Press. Copyright 1953). Additional thanks are extended to Alva Davis for permission to use data from his doctoral dissertation, *A Word Atlas of the Great Lakes States* (University of Michigan, 1948), and to The Ronald Press Company for permission to reprint material contained in W. Nelson Francis' *The Structure of American English* (Copyright 1958).

Further acknowledgments go to the American Dialect Society for permitting me to quote from articles by Albert Marckwardt, David Reed and myself.

C. E. R.

# *Foreword*

Since the inauguration of the Linguistic Atlas project in 1930, American scholars have accumulated impressive evidence on the regional and social variations in American English, on the causes of these variations, and on the directions of change. This evidence is interesting in its own right; it is highly useful to the sociologist and the historian; it is indispensable to those charged with the teaching of English in American schools.

Unfortunately, this information is far less accessible than it should be. *The Linguistic Atlas of New England* and its accompanying *Handbook* were out of print for a long time and are likely to be found chiefly in research libraries. Moreover, its data is not self-interpreting, even for scholars in other fields; in fact, among the sociolinguistic studies available, only Labov's examination of /ai/ and /au/ on Martha's Vineyard can be said to have made serious use of it. The *Atlas of the Middle and South Atlantic States* moves slowly toward publication; but again it will be designed primarily for the specialist. For the Atlantic Seaboard there are three books interpreting the data for a wider reading public: Kurath's *Word Geography of the Eastern United States,* E. Bagby Atwood's *Survey of Verb Forms in the Eastern United States,* and Kurath's and my *Pronunciation of English in the Atlantic States.* But these hardly extend much further westward than the upper reaches of the Ohio Valley.

For the rest of the country the situation is somewhat better than it was when the first edition of this book appeared. Harold Allen's *Linguistic Atlas of the Upper Midwest* (1973–75) has now been published. Albert H. Marckwardt, before his death, had worked out plans for editing the *Linguistic Atlas of the North-Central States,* and these are now being carried out by Marckwardt's associates. The work will be largely interpretative, though the complex process of editing will make available the full phonetic data of unretouched field records on microfilm and Xerox. Elizabeth Bright's *Word Geography of California and Nevada* has provided an overview—if tantalizingly brief—of part of the Pacific Coast. And with field work complete in the Gulf States, Oklahoma and Missouri, as well as in part of the Maritimes, we will soon have data for a historical interpretation of American dialects. But the very bulk of available material makes the task of interpretation difficult; even the interpretative volumes for the Atlantic Seaboard are not designed for the laity. Summaries of the evidence, such as the one on which Alva L. Davis and I have been working desultorily over the past two decades, are likely to be on too large a scale for the ready reference of the average reader. Finally, the ability to present a sound interpretation of dialectology in a clear style is rare indeed, and most of those who possess this ability are fully committed to other writing projects for some years to come.

Both professionally and personally, I am happy to see the revised second edition of this work by Carroll Reed, a friend of mine for more than thirty-five years. As one of Kurath's students, he has had incomparable training. He has had the awakening experience of field work in two different languages—Pennsylvania German and American English. His book reflects not only his bilingual experience but the fresh perspective of an area whose variations are little known. Finally, he has provided a generous sheaf of well-designed maps—the most effective way of indicating regional variation.

In short, this is a good first book for any reader who has just become aware of dialect variations. With this at hand, it should be easier to use such a pedagogically oriented work as Roger Shuy's *Discovering American Dialects* (Champaign, Illinois, the National Council of Teachers of English, 1967) and the mass of sociolinguistic studies that have been conducted in the past decade, to read with profit the longer scholarly treatments, the growing body of scholarly articles, and ultimately the regional atlases themselves. As custodian of the Atlas archives for the Atlantic Seaboard under the auspices of the American Council of Learned Societies, and now also executor of Marckwardt's plans for the North-Central States, I am always happy to see our materials used by responsible scholars. But I am even more happy now than I was when his first edition appeared, to know that Professor Reed's book will continue to be accessible to those who need it.

Raven I. McDavid, Jr., *Editor in Chief,*
*Linguistic Atlas of the Middle and South Atlantic States*

# *Author's Note on the Second Edition*

Ten years after the construction of my first edition it has become clear that certain changes and additions are needed, notably the new chapters on Black English and Urban Dialects. Further entries in the "selected" bibliography have also been added.

Readers of the first edition have frequently indicated their pleasure with my use of nontechnical language. Some linguists, however, have deplored the rather imprecise phonetic spellings adapted from standard English. For this elite group then, I am listing below some broad transcriptions in symbols of the International Phonetic Alphabet for items whose pronunciation may be obscure in my perhaps overly popular renditions.

*Chapter 5:*
Chicago [hɑɪ tɑɪm] "high time,"
[fʌɪt], [mʌɪt] "fight, might."
Galveston [ha: ta:m] "high time,"
[fʌɪt], [mʌɪt] "fight, might."
Northern [rɑʊnd] "round," [hɑʊs] or [hʌʊs] "house."
Southern [ræʊnd] "round," [hʌʊs] or [hɑʊs] "house."
Brooklynese, etc. [bʌɪd, hʌɪd, kʌɪl] "bird, heard, curl."
"r-coloring" [wɔ$^{r}$s] "wash."
Southern [wʌɪš] or [wɑɪš] "wash."
*ah* [a] *aw* [ɔ].
[hɚi] or [hʌri] or [hɑri] "hurry."

*Chapter 10:*
California [ɛg] vs. [e$^{I}$g] "egg."
New York [tʌɪdi tʌɪd] "thirty third."
[fo$^{U}$əθ flo$^{U}$ə] "fourth floor."
[kɛ:ə] "care," [bo$^{U}$əd] "board."
Boston [pa:k ðə ka: rɪn ðə pa:k] "park the car in the park."

CHAPTER *1*

# *Introduction to Dialect Study*

What is language? Among the various activities of men everywhere there is at least one common feature of culture which appears to be indispensable—language. It is recognized primarily as a complicated system of signaling facilitated by the mechanism of the voice. It is acquired over the years by contact with other people and not without considerable effort. Above all, it enables us to transmit information, to store up knowledge, and to formulate directives for the governing of human affairs. General definitions of language vary, but linguists and anthropologists more or less agree that it is "a purely arbitrary system of vocal symbols by means of which human beings interact."[1]

All known peoples possess language. Many, of course, have no means of representing their speech in the form of writing. In fact, some authorities estimate that there are more than two thousand languages in the world which have never been reduced to writing. Writing, therefore, must be considered a secondary

[1] For further definitions and sources see: C. E. Reed, "What is Linguistics?" *German Quarterly,* XXV (Jan., 1952), 16–25; and G. L. Trager, *The Field of Linguistics* (*Studies in Linguistics,* Occasional papers, No. 1). Norman, Okla.: Battenburg Press, 1949.

manifestation of language. Likewise, other such representations and devices exist, some rather crude and some more elaborate; gesture, facial expressions, code signals, weather vanes, and road signs are among them.

But what then is a dialect? This is a more difficult question to answer than the first. For languages normally consist of dialects, or special varieties of usage within the range of a given linguistic system, according to the social or geographical disposition of its speakers. Linguists speak of English, German, and Dutch as "Germanic dialects," since they derive from a common parent and are closely related. High and Low German are known as "German dialects," since they are associated with the national language shared by their speakers.[2] Thus, we can see that *a* language may be defined either on a historical basis, as a collection of related dialects, or on a political basis, as a collection of related dialects in a given area, often encompassing a single nationality. Strictly speaking, different languages are not mutually intelligible; different dialects of the same language ordinarily are mutually intelligible (although there are some notable exceptions, such as certain varieties of Chinese).

We shall assume, however, that British and American English are collections of dialects within the English language, which we shall speak of as "British dialects" ("Scottish," "Irish," etc., as the case may be) and "American dialects," respectively, in line with certain geographical considerations. At the same time, we shall keep in mind the fact that the English language is, in another sense, a dialect derivate of a Germanic language branch which, in turn, is descended from the great Indo-European parent stock.

Dialects may be geographical in the sense of being spoken by people living in certain areas. Although the boundaries of

[2] Low German consists of those dialects spoken in the lowlands of northern Germany. High German is spoken in the southern half of the country (as well as in Switzerland and Austria). Standard written German is derived from several High German dialects.

such dialects are often clearly limited by certain differences in speech habits, the transition from one dialect area to another may also be very gradual, so that differences can only be noted between centers of widely separated areas, or centers of maximum difference. Older settlements, such as those existing on the continent of Europe, often show sharp and extensive differences, while colonial areas, such as those found in the United States, tend to be more homogenous. Dialects of colonial areas are also more often uniform over a wider area than those of the smaller areas of a mother country, and it is for this reason that people living in a relatively new territory (such as the Pacific Northwest) rarely notice a significant feature of dialect difference in the speech around them.

Personal differences are frequently more striking and are easily mistaken for the systematic type of difference which can be assigned to dialects. Linguists call the speech of individuals their "idiolects." Each person makes use of his language in a way peculiar to his individual history. Insofar as he does not conform exactly to the speech habits of others with a similar history, he is marked by the features of his own "idiolect." Thus we say: "Oh, I thought that was Bill talking," "He talks like John," "Jane talks with a kind of a lisp," or "I can always recognize him by the tone of his voice," etc.

But dialects (which are composites of idiolects) may also be classified according to criteria other than geographical ones. For instance, a clearly marked social or economic class organizes and makes use of language according to its own requirements. In class-conscious Europe this is much more the case than in the United States. Bernard Shaw illustrated the nature of class dialects very well in his play *Pygmalion,* where he had a professor of phonetics make a lady out of a poor flower girl simply by teaching her to speak (as well as to act) in accordance with the conventions of an upper-class society.

Within a given area, the amount of education received by various people goes hand in hand either with class status or with the age-group involved, since fashions change in education, and the tendency has long been in the direction of an increase in educational influences, even among the most underprivileged. The dialect of persons having abandoned their education at a given stage, therefore, often tends to retain characteristics of that particular stage. In areas where speech education is retarded, a wise politician will gauge his use of language to fit the level of his constituents. His folksy speech may have special appeal in certain areas, but woe be unto him if he uses rough speech in addressing an educated audience!

Attempts to live beyond one's linguistic means, however, frequently result in the use of ridiculously pompous speech, or even *unnaturally* ungrammatical forms (naturally ungrammatical forms are frequent enough!). Thus, some people find it elegant to say: "He came with John and *I,*" rather than using the proper form *me,* since they have learned that it is both impolite and "wrong" to say: "Me and John came with him." Similar motivation can be found for the permanent mutilation of foreign words adopted by speakers of only one language (monolinguals); for example, the French word *écrevisse* was changed to *crayfish* and *crawfish,* even though the creature so named was hardly any sort of "fish," and western Americans know it better by the term *crawdad.* Likewise, *cold-slaw* has resulted from tinkering with the word *cole-slaw,* an American-Dutch spelling for *kool sla* "chopped cabbage."

It is through constant use and modification on the part of its speakers, however, that the forms of a language change. By the mixing together of dialects, new conditions are constantly being set up. Moreover, linguistic scientists have noted that languages possess certain formal aspects which tend towards regularity. Such regularity, while exhibiting a principle of economy in the utilization of linguistic resources, does not necessarily mean simplicity; any language can be exceedingly complicated for a person who has to learn it as a second tongue. Nor is the complicated structure of a language an index of any given cultural status; in fact, many languages of culturally primitive people are unbelievably complex. The grammatical intricacies of Eskimo, for instance, represent a case in point.

All languages change with use, but they do not change uniformly in time and space. Most languages, therefore, contain remnants of archaic usage as well as certain odd innovations. Thus, English has adjectives like *molten, cloven,* and *sodden,* which were once verb forms, but have been replaced by the "regular" types, *melted, cleaved,* and *seethed.* By observing the archaic language of the English Bible, for example, we can see how far this sort of change has gone. When we meet a man from the Virginia mountains who says "he might have *holp* me" (for "he might have *helped* me"), we must not hasten to declare that the man's (admittedly nonstandard) speech is but a corrupted form of standard English. In fact, if we consult the *Oxford English Dictionary* on such matters, we often find that the forms suspected to be "corrupted" were once quite "correct" in the King's English.

Western Americans use the word *cuss* frequently enough but seldom realize that it is a borrowed form of the word *curse* in accordance with the pronunciation of once-elegant Yankee speech, where the "dropped *r*" was a mark of distinction. The term *hoss* for *horse* is generally considered folksy, however, and is used more in a spirit of levity than anything else. Obsolescent speech forms are preserved with great irregularity then, according to the dialect involved, and may be used by the linguist as a means of learning more about earlier structural stages of a language; such archaisms are, in a manner of speaking, fossils in the tar pit of human culture.

In order to understand the nature and origin of conditions prevailing in dialects today, therefore, we must learn to understand the circumstances which fostered them. American English dialects must be observed as an aspect of cultural history. We need to study the historical forms of the English language as they appear in earlier documents, and we must keep in mind the social, economic, and geographical changes experienced by

English speakers. Part of our attention must be devoted to inspecting the works of great writers like Shakespeare, who not only used the English language in its various stylistic forms, but who also knew some of the problems involved in adjusting it to fit the changing times. Another fund of information, of course, can be gleaned from the numerous works of grammarians, whose efforts were generally committed to reducing the language to rule.

The fruits of comparative language study supply still further clues to the history of a language. Yet one of the richest sources we have is the evidence furnished by present-day dialects. Within the last hundred years a new science, known as dialectology, or linguistic geography, has made its appearance in the field of cultural history. Its methods are briefly as follows: A concise questionnaire is constructed for the purpose of testing speakers of a language as to the way their particular dialect makes use of that language. These speakers are chosen on the basis of their economic, social, religious, or educational background, and are sought in both rural and urban areas. When enough speakers have been sampled in the required areas, their responses can be recorded graphically on a map, so that any variation in usage can be observed quite readily. Geographical deviations, involving groups of different features, then permit us to draw "isoglosses" on the map. These vaguely resemble isobars on a weather map, but they serve to mark somewhat sharper differences than the arbitrary point of transition symbolized in the weather map. See the adjoining figure.

In older speech areas, as already indicated, dialect areas are usually easy to identify, particularly with the aid of linguistic geography. The eastern part of the United States, if studied in this way, reveals a number of "isogloss bundles" marking distinctly the various dialect boundaries. As one looks westward, however, and encounters fairly recently commingled areas of settlement, the identification of specific dialect areas becomes impossible, so that the preponderance of certain forms of language over others becomes a matter of statistical dispersion,

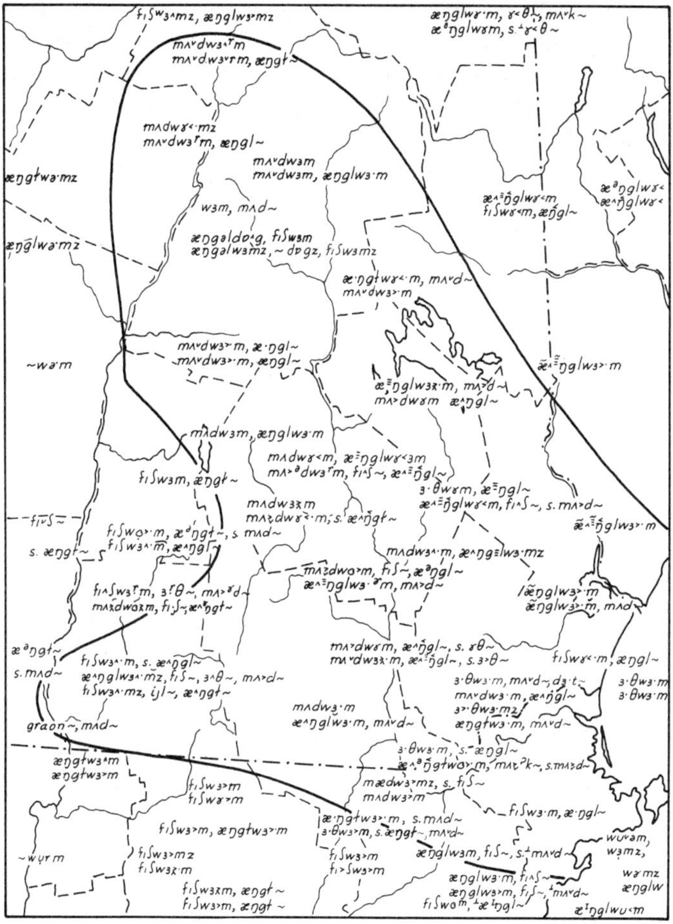

Outer limits of the term mudworm "earthworm" in New England.
[From: The Linguistic Atlas of New England, Vol. I, map 236]

and our linguistic map resembles more a scattergram than a series of mutually exclusive areas. As we shall see later, however, it is still possible there to observe tendencies that reveal those directions a language may take in seeking regularity at some future date. Observation of language behavior in the past gives us important information on the probability of future conditions.

CHAPTER 2

# Colonial English

The English language was established in the British Isles (according to one tradition, at least) sometime after the year 449 A.D., when various Continental tribes—chiefly Angles, Saxons, Jutes, and Frisians—came to "protect," settle, and eventually conquer what was later to be called England (i.e., "Angleland"), particularly in the eastern and southern part. From the very earliest period to the present time, linguistic differences have existed here among what has always been a mutually intelligible set of related (Germanic) dialects. The Scandinavian invasion and settlement of England, from the eighth to the tenth centuries, also had an effect on the subsequent history of the English language, particularly in the dialects of northern and eastern England.

The Norman French invasion of England in 1066 effected still further changes in the linguistic situation—both directly and indirectly; directly by the fact that the introduction of French customs and ways, especially in official matters, brought with it an influx of French expressions; indirectly in that the temporary abandonment of English as an official language permitted the various dialects to develop naturally in their everyday use by ordinary people.

By the time of the Renaissance, the English language had regained supremacy as a standard for the realm, but the vicissitudes of history continued to leave their marks on the speech of nobles, tradesmen, and peasants alike. After the introduction of printing, scholars and literate persons of various sorts attempted to formulate rules and educate the public taste for a standard language which could be taught in schools, written in books, and recorded in dictionaries. From the untiring efforts of such people, a noble heritage was developed, a vehicle of expression that has produced one of the world's richest literatures.

The time of Shakespeare (1564–1616) antedated only slightly the period of early colonization in America. For that reason it will be illuminating for us here to examine the kind of English spoken at that time, since it was during the next century and a half that various types of English then current were established in the Colonies. From such early settlements, patterns were established which had a profound and lasting effect on the nature of modern American dialects.

Shakespeare's speech—as exhibited in his works, at least—seems to have represented rather well the cultivated usage of Elizabethan England, particularly in the area around London; and what is more, it was sensitive to social levels. The King James Bible on the other hand, published in 1611, gives us a picture of an elegant form of speech more typical of the previous century. In the Bible, for example, *thou* is singular and *ye* is plural, and the objective forms are *thee* and *you,* respectively. In Shakespeare, *thou* and *you* are both used in the singular (*you* also in the plural, of course) according to the relationship expressed by the speakers involved and in keeping with a medieval tradition of gentility. But *you* and *ye* are not distinguished grammatically from one another.

Again, the Bible uses *-eth* consistently in such forms as *he loveth,* etc., while Shakespeare uses *-eth* and *-es* both, more or less as rhythm demands, thus:

> The quality of mercy is not strain'd,
> It dropp*eth* as the gentle rain from heaven

Upon the place beneath: it is twice blest;
It bless*eth* him that giv*es* and him that tak*es*.
(*Merchant of Venice,* IV. i. 184–187.)

In fact, the poetic *-eth* seems to have been an archaism or an affectation even in Shakespeare's time.

Likewise, in the Biblical language of the sixteenth century we find the words "Our Father *which* art in heaven," whereas a century later this would have been expressed: "Our Father *who* art in heaven."

People reading the Bible today are struck by the odd verb forms encountered there; for instance, *blowed, growed, shrinked, brake, spake,* and *holp*. In American speech of the present day some of these are still current, but they are no longer representative of educated usage. We call them "substandard" or, to avoid any trace of bias, "nonstandard." Shakespeare used some of these, as well as forms like *have took, have strove, hath wrote, have swam,* etc. And of course the grammatical sins of modern times had not yet been scourged by the mathematical logic of later centuries, so that it was possible then to say *more better, most unkindest, worser,* and such things as *I cannot go no further* or *nor is this my nose neither*. Multiple negatives, indeed, had long been "proper" English usage, serving merely to support and intensify rather than to cancel one another. An Elizabethan would scarcely have raised an eyebrow upon hearing such an expression as *they don't know nothing!* In fact, it was even possible for Shakespeare to commit such seeming "errors" as the following:

All debts are cleared *between you and I*.
(*Merchant of Venice,* III. ii. 319–320.)

. . . should I find them
So saucy with *the hand of she* here
(*Antony and Cleopatra,* III. xiii. 97–98.)

And yet no man *like he* doth grieve my heart.
(*Romeo and Juliet,* III. v. 84.)

On the matter of pronunciation let us consider the following famous passage from *As You Like It* (II. vii. 138–166):

All the world's a *stage,*
And all the men and women merely *players:*
*They* have their exits and their entrances;
And *one* man in his *time plays* many *parts,*
His acts being seven *ages.* At first the infant,
Mewling and puking in the nurse's *arms.*
And then the *whining* school-boy, with his satchel
And *shining* morning *face,* creeping like *snail*
Unwillingly to school. And then the *lover,*
*Sighing like* furnace, with a woeful ballad
*Made* to his mistress' *eyebrow.* Then a soldier,
Full of *strange* oaths and *bearded* like the *pard,*
Jealous in honor, *sudden* and quick in *quarrel,*
Seeking the *bubble reputation*
Even in the cannon's *mouth.* And then the *justice,*
In *fair round* belly with good *capon lined,*
With *eyes* severe, and *beard* of formal *cut,*
Full of *wise* saws and modern instances;
And so he *plays* his *part.* The sixth *age* shifts
Into the *lean* and slipper'd pantaloon,
With spectacles on nose and pouch on *side,*
His youthful hose, well *saved,* a world too *wide*
For his *shrunk* shank; and his big manly voice,
Turning *again* toward *childish* treble, *pipes*
And whistles in his *sound.* Last scene of all,
That ends this *strange* eventful history,
Is second *childishness* and mere oblivion,
Sans teeth, sans *eyes,* sans *taste,* sans everything.[1]

[1] Various scholars have used this selection from Shakespeare in order to illustrate his pronunciation: e.g., Helge Kökeritz, *Shakespeare's Pronunciation* (New Haven: Yale University Press, 1953). The author follows a system given by A. H. Marckwardt, *American English* (New York: Oxford University Press, Inc., 1958), pp. 188–189.

The vowels in the italicized syllables were pronounced as follows:

(1) *a* in *stage, ages, face, made, strange, reputation, capon, saved, taste* was similar to *a* in our words *sad* and *mad.*

(2) *ai, ay, ey* in *players, they, plays, snail, fair,* and *again* were pronounced like present-day *eye.*

(3) *a* before *r* in *parts, arms, pard* and *quarrel* was pronounced more like modern *a* in *cat* or *mat.*

(4) *ea* in *beard* and *lean* was pronounced like modern *ay* in *day.*

(5) *u, o* in *one, lover, sudden, bubble, justice, cut, shrunk* were pronounced like the *oo* of our word *look* or the *u* of *full* and *put.*

(6) *i* in *time, whining, shining, sighing, like, lined, wise, side, wide, childish, pipes* was not an *áh-ee* as it is today, but rather something like *úh-ee.*

(7) *ou, ow* in *eyebrow, mouth, round, sound* was pronounced as *úh-oo.*

The vowels *i* and *ou/ow* (6, 7) are still pronounced the same way in some English dialects; they represent an intermediate stage between their older English pronunciations—as *ee* and *oo* (preserved in modern Scottish)—and the modern rendition.

The sound of *a* before *r* (3) is preserved in the speech of Boston, although the *r* sound itself is now generally lost before consonants or at the end of the word. An *e* before *r* was similarly pronounced in many words, and a subsequent struggle between dialects has resulted in a split between British and American *clerk* (as "clark" vs. "clerk"), *derby* (as "darby" vs. "derby"), *Berkeley* (as "barkly" vs. "berkly"), or the American forms *varsity* vs. *university.* Other examples of such differences are known from early records, as well as from literary forms of rustic speech—as found, for example, in ballads. Thus, we occasionally encounter *sartin* for "certain," *marcy* for "mercy," *sarvice* for "service," *tarnal* for "eternal," *sarpent* for "serpent," *varmint* for "vermin," etc.; the words *parson* (with its special meaning) and *smart,* however, are accepted pronunciations of "person" and (former) "smert," respectively, and the personal names *Clark* and *Sargent* are common enough alongside of the words *clerk* and *sergeant,* from which they are derived. In Shakespeare, then, there existed an intermediate vowel—between *a*(*r*) and *e*(*r*)—and the words *convert, art, depart, desert,* and *part* were evidently perfect rhymes. Shakespeare also rhymed *herd* with *beard* and *granting* with *wanting*. The original forms of "Goosey-goosey *gander,* whither shall I *wander*" also rhymed, though they no longer do in American English.

If the passage given from *As You Like It* is now read with the values noted, plus the addition of a trilled *r,* a sensitive listener may declare: "Why, that sounds like Irish English!" Just so, for the characteristics which Americans associate with Irish English are tied to the immigrant variety of speech that has been made popular by dialogue artists and lyric tenors. Irish English, of course, along with other English dialects, preserves many of the traits of earlier English that we tend to associate with the age of Shakespeare.

Dialect contention in such matters as the pronunciation of *clerk* extended to other features of English well up into the eighteenth century, and the repercussions of this struggle were felt on both sides of the Atlantic. Thus, the principal speakers of educated classes differed sharply on the pronunciation of *oi*. The cultivated use of the sound "eye" in such words as *boil, poison, hoist, join,* and *spoil,* is now reflected only in rustic speech in the United States, simply because another standard has taken its place. Fixed phrases are then used occasionally as a means of epitomizing certain rough-and-ready people, or in the fulfillment of a type of jargon, such as nautical terminology. We may crack a knowing smile and say: "Name yer pizen, pardner!" or confidently shout: "Heist the jib there, mate!" (In criminal argot, of course, the term "heist" is strictly de rigueur.)

Another illustration of dialect change in British English as it affected the development of American dialects is seen in the so-called dropped *r.* As early as the fifteenth century we find evidence that British dialects of southern English were dropping the traditional *r* before consonants or at the end of words. This had become fashionable, even in educated circles, by the seventeenth century, when the American Colonies received their greatest influx. More northerly English dialects, however, retained the *r* until after this period, so that the earliest American settlements, showing the strong imprint of southern English dialects, were marked by the characteristic loss of *r,* while later settlements, extending further inland, retained the *r* sound. By far the largest part of the United States today continues to use this *r* in all its forms, and this is a legacy of those former frontier settlements.

Cities of the East Coast long maintained their contact with London, and the Southern gentry continued to go to England for their education. Hence, the *r*-less speech was not only perpetuated for a long time in New England and in the South, especially in the larger cities, but it gained in prestige as a standard to which people are "born" or, at least, "bred." Consequently, a number of *r*-less words have crept into the other dialects: *bobwire* "barbed wire," *bust* "burst," *cuss* "curse," *gal* "girl," etc.

Similar provincialisms of this type include the southern British forms *critter* "creature," *chaw* "chew," *east* "yeast," *hant* "haunt," *yelk* "yolk," and *tetched* "touched." In some areas of the American South, for instance, these particular forms are extremely common.

It can be said that the English language was much more flexible in Shakespeare's time than it is today. The influence of education was less prominent, and, of course, the written word had an extremely limited circulation. There was less concern with linguistic matters; "international" dictionaries, grammars, spellers, etc., were almost nonexistent, particularly in Colonial America. And schooling was, for the greater part, left in the hands of private tutors, usually poor ministers of divers origins and ability. Since the mass of the population immigrating to

America was relatively uneducated, the spoken language easily determined the standard in any given locality. Economic conditions, as we shall see, were then responsible for the implanting and stratification of dialects which were to affect the course of the English language in America for centuries to come.

CHAPTER 3

# Eastern Settlement

By 1700 a relatively small part of the original thirteen Colonies had been settled: Eastern Massachusetts, Connecticut, the Hudson Valley, New Jersey, the Philadelphia area, Delaware, eastern Maryland and Virginia, and a small area around Charleston, South Carolina, contained the bulk of the population. Most of this, of course, was concentrated in the larger cities—Boston, New York, Philadelphia, and Charleston.

During the next seventy-five years these settlements were extended as far west as the Allegheny and Appalachian Mountains, and southward to include the piedmont areas of the Carolinas. Northern New England, western New York, Georgia, and Florida were still a vast wilderness.

New England and most of the areas of the central Atlantic Coast were populated largely by people from the eastern and southern part of England. Western New England seems to have received a number of emigrants from the area directly north and northwest of London, and settlers from northern England were also to be found here. Scotch-Irish (Ulsterites) soon joined this group, but they were most numerous along the frontiers. Very little documentary information is actually available on population origins of that time, but linguistic evidence, as we shall see, is abundant and fruitful.

During the first half of the eighteenth century a large group of Germans came to America and settled solidly throughout southeastern Pennsylvania. These are now known—inaccurately—as the Pennsylvania Dutch. They speak their transplanted German dialects even to the present day; their speech is really nothing more than a composite of dialects spoken in and around the Rhenish Palatinate (some cities of which are Worms, Kaiserslautern, Speyer, Heidelberg, and Mannheim). The Germans settled as far west as the Susquehanna River, where a new wave of Scotch-Irish caught up with them and began to work its way towards the Southwest and the West, following the frontier.

A group of Welsh also settled in an area just west of Philadelphia. Along with indentured English and poor immigrants of various sorts, however, the Germans and Scotch-Irish were responsible for cultural patterns, including language patterns, which eventually became established in the American "Midland" areas. A good deal of the picturesque "mountain" speech of those regions south of the Ohio River reflects the influence of these people. Their hardiness and probably the enduring qualities of their speech are commemorated in the fame of such people as Abraham Lincoln, Jefferson Davis, Andrew Jackson, David Crockett, and a host of others. These "Midlanders" represented a cultural block of democratic free men, standing between the less variegated "Northerners" and the class-conscious "Southerners."

Partly for religious reasons and partly because the economy of the country so dictated, the conditions relating to population were different in the South than in the North. The landed gentry of the old South continued to send their sons to England for their education. Indentured white labor was soon replaced by black slave labor, and by degrees the South became a series of huge single-crop plantations, the first great product of which was tobacco. "Poor whites," including underprivileged or exiled unfortunates of one kind or another, became inhabitants of the back-hills and swamps. The predominantly Negro population took on forms of speech used by the white laboring classes, and this tendency was augmented by the contributions of their white employers. The variations which were then developed remained a function of social stratification, population mixture among immigrants, and the cross-breeding of internal migration. A merchant group, the speech of which now ranges somewhere between that of the gentry and the poorer classes, seems to have established itself in the larger cities, with corresponding local character. It is this group that has expanded most rapidly, in smaller towns of the inland South and then extensively further to the west, as far as southeastern Texas, for example.

It should be noted, however, that, with the possible exception of Gullah dialects in isolated areas of the Carolina Coast, there are seldom any unique patterns which would distinguish Negro from white speakers. In more or less out-of-the-way communities, the type of speech used will bear the stamp of regionalism, whether the speakers themselves are white or Negro. There is no truth in any claim that a physical feature—the shape of a man's face or the color of his skin—has any direct correlation with the way in which a language is articulated. An effect of racial segregation, however, is to create conditioned varieties of English that are characteristic of the segregated group, so that the popular identification of speech on racial lines is not always without substance. Any group of people is apt to develop its own peculiar linguistic stamp because of its geographical, cultural, or economic coherence. This is especially noticeable in areas settled by speakers of foreign languages, where pockets of alien culture may persist for long periods. Allusion has already been made above, for example, to the Pennsylvania Germans. In the same way, groups of Scandinavians, French, or Latin Americans could also be cited.

CHAPTER 4

# *Eastern Words*

Map 1 (p. 85) is adapted from one devised by Hans Kurath, of the University of Michigan, in his book *A Word Geography of the Eastern United States*.[1] Here the speech areas of what was once Colonial America are defined on the basis of material gathered by fieldworkers for the Linguistic Atlas of the United States and Canada.[2]

It will be seen that two prominent sets of isoglosses divide the Eastern States into three large areas. These are called Northern, Midland, and Southern. Each of the areas can then be broken down into sub-areas having definite dialect characteristics delineated by the isoglosses shown. In the following chapters we shall want to keep this map clearly in mind, for it is with special reference to the areas illustrated here that the features peculiar to other regions will be described. Particular attention should be focused on the western part of the section shown on

[1] Ann Arbor: University of Michigan Press, 1949.

[2] An extensive account of this project, with its various offshoots and ramifications, may be found in the following two articles: R. I. McDavid, Jr., and V. G. McDavid. "Regional Linguistic Atlases in the United States," *Orbis,* V (June, 1956), 349–386; and E. B. Atwood. "The Methods of American Dialectology," *Zeitschrift für Mundartforschung,* XXX (Oct., 1963), 1–30.

Map 1, since this area was directly responsible for transmitting speech to sections of the country further west.

In this connection one should note the peculiar contours of the Midland area, the manner in which it increases toward the West, and the corresponding restrictions of the Southern area. As we shall later discover, the Northern area dips southward as it extends towards the West and plays a more prominent role there than this map might lead us to assume.

Careful scrutiny of the map reveals the fact that certain topographical and economically strategic factors have been at work. Areas 2, 6, and 7 include Boston, New York, and Philadelphia, respectively. Areas 3, 5, 7, 8, 9, 10, and 17 are associated with river valleys representing water potential for power, navigation, drainage, etc. The line separating Midland from Southern speech follows generally the first great mountain barrier, which was sufficient to retard inland migration from the Southern Piedmont until the Germans and Scotch-Irish in Pennsylvania could move southwestward and settle in the valleys there.

Isolation has played a part in the development of a peninsular area (14) (called Delmarva after the states involved—*Del*aware, *Mar*yland and *V*irgini*a*), and other such instances will be encountered elsewhere, but on a smaller scale.

The dialect of the coastal areas of New England has remained stable for a long time, contributing to no great part of the Northern area as it expanded westward. But since this region was, from the first, oriented in the direction of the sea, its importance will be apparent when we examine the speech of the West Coast. As a sea-going people, the inhabitants of coastal New England played a notable role, for example, in the exploration, settlement, and economic development of such areas as those around San Francisco, the lower Columbia River, and Puget Sound.

Because people living in larger cities usually tend to migrate, if at all, to other cities, we will note the fact that one-time New Yorkers and their offspring are well represented in West Coast ports. By the same token the city of Chicago will be found to have absorbed a large part of the people (or their descendants) who moved westward from Boston and New York. As in San Francisco and Seattle, however, a very complicated process of population mixture or accretion has taken place in Chicago because of the great fire of 1871, after which a good many descendants of the original settlers moved to cities further west. And the development of the railroads during the latter part of the nineteenth century then further disturbed such settlement patterns.

Rural communities contribute constantly to the population of towns and cities. The reverse is not often true, but the cultural and economic effects of cities on rural groups are enormous. So we may expect to find more uniformity in the speech of more recent American cities than among the outlying areas. Folk speech will be augmented there, of course, by contributions from the country. The cultural influence of the city will be felt in the country, particularly when it comes to technical matters. Both rural and urban populations generally reveal definite educational levels, the most advanced of which would tend to cultivate uniform speech characteristics throughout increasingly larger areas.

While the divisions shown on Map 1 are set up on the basis of vocabulary distinctions, Kurath's more recently published material on pronunciation and grammar readily confirms the disposition of dialect areas seen here. Since that material is exceedingly complex in nature, it is practical for us to examine first the lexical items offered here, so that we may acquire an over-all picture of dialect areas and then proceed to other elements of speech, including those which have been given special attention in studies made by individual scholars.

The Northern area is set apart from the Midland area on the basis of the terms *whiffletree/whippletree* "singletree," *pail,* and *darning needle* "dragonfly." The terms *stoneboat* "stone sled" and *teeter(board)* "teeter-totter" also tend to reach their limits at this point, except that eastern New England (1, 2) has (*stone*) *drag* more often than *stoneboat.* If the Hudson Valley (5, 6) is excluded, we may add to these the terms *spider* "frying pan," *skaffle* "scaffold" (in a barn), and *buttry* "pantry."

Including the Hudson Valley (5, 6), but again excluding eastern New England (1, 2), we may add the term *stoop* "porch," which is of Holland Dutch origin.

As a unique area, eastern New England has, in addition to *stone drag,* the terms *belly-bump/belly-bumper* "sliding face down on a sled," *sour-milk cheese* "cottage cheese," and *whicker* "whinny," as contrasted to the terms used in other Northern areas. Some of these terms, of course, are used in parts of the Midland and the South also.

Another part of the Northern area having common characteristics is the Hudson Valley, where Holland Dutch influence has been strong. New York City forms the nucleus of this section, but various unique terms are used as far north as Albany. The words *suppawn* "corn mush," (*hay*) *barrack* "hay stack," and *pot cheese* "cottage cheese," for example, are included here. Around New York City *skimerton/skimilton* is a word describing the mock serenade held in connection with a wedding (many westerners know it as a *charivari,* pronounced *shivaree*). In the Eastern States the familiar Middle Western and Western word *teeter-totter,* moreover, is restricted largely to the Hudson Valley area. The distribution of these terms, along with place names containing the Dutch word *kill* "brook," follows generally the limits of Dutch settlement in New York State. One Dutch word, however, has been carried far beyond the original settlement to include also southern New England and most of New Jersey, as well as a good part of eastern Pennsylvania; this is the term *cruller,* used to describe an unraised sweet doughnut. As is usually the case when competing forms overlap on the edges of dialect areas, semantic differentiation is here very productive. A person needs only to inquire in New England about the meaning of a word like *cruller* in order to become embroiled in seemingly endless argument as to the meaning of both this word and *doughnut*—with respect to its shape and recipe.

In addition to being set apart from both Northern and Southern areas by the absence of features according to which these areas are distinguished, the Midland area is represented by terms like *sook!* (a call to cows), *snake feeder* "dragonfly," and *I want off!* "I want to get off!" The last two of these correspond to German usage and are an obvious indication of the part played by the Pennsylvania Germans in this region. Nearly coincident geographically with these terms are the expressions *blinds* "roller shades" and *bawl* (of a calf); *poke* "paper bag" and *sugar tree* "maple tree" are used in the same area with the exception of southeastern Pennsylvania, where the German word *toot* "paper bag" is used also in English.

Other German loan expressions may be noted: *school leaves out* "school lets out," *overhead* "loft" (of the barn), *flitch* "side of bacon," and *thick milk* "curdled milk" are found in all but the very northern part of Pennsylvania; *flannel cakes/flannen cakes* "pancakes," *ponhaws* "scrapple," and *till the time* "by the time" begin in Pennsylvania and continue into the mountain valleys of Maryland, West Virginia, and Virginia, where *till the time* competes with the general Southern folk form *agin' the time*.

Extended even further southwestward are *rainworm* "earthworm," *vootsie* (call to the pigs), and *saddle horse* "near horse" (of a team). Throughout the northern part of the Midland area, the term *smearcase* "cottage cheese" has spread to places where formerly the product itself was little known. It is interesting to note that the Dutch term *pot cheese* and the German *smearcase* were received quite differently in nearby areas: *pot cheese* was not borrowed extensively, but *Dutch cheese* was coined in adjacent areas to describe the product by its source; *smearcase* was borrowed widely, but a number of people in West Virginia —in accordance with the popular concept of Pennsylvania Germans—took up the term *Dutch cheese* in reference to their German neighbors.

The Scotch-Irish settlements of western Pennsylvania often share the idiosyncrasies of the Pennsylvania Germans in their use of English and, as such, form a solid bastion within the

Midland area. Their early influence is seen in a series of isoglosses (Map 7, p. 91) for the words *hap* "quilt/counterpane," (*hay*) *doodle* "hay pile," and *drooth* "drought."

Various other subdivisions of the Midland area can also be illustrated, one of which is the interesting southwestern Midland section deep in the heart of the Appalachian Mountains. Popular belief tends to regard the people in this area as "Southern"—as if the division of dialects in America were somehow a function of the Civil War era. The Mason-Dixon line, separating Pennsylvania and Maryland, actually coincides with few isoglosses, albeit they are very striking; hence we find *you-all* "you" (plural), (*corn*) *shucks* "husks," and *light bread* "wheat bread" as terms used to the south of the line, whereas *you-uns* (western Pennsylvania), *youse* (New Jersey and eastern Pennsylvania), and *you* (general everywhere), as well as (*corn*) *husks* and *wheat bread* or *white bread* (occasionally also *raised* or *riz bread* on the coast) are used in the Northern area.

The Southern area itself includes only the southeastern coast and slope (14–18 on Map 1). The Virginia Piedmont section is unique in many ways; here we find the terms *line horse/wheel horse* "near horse," *cow house* "cow barn," and *cuppin* "cow pen." The piedmont areas of Virginia and South Carolina share the expressions *cooter* "turtle," *corn house* "corn crib," and *croker sack* "burlap sack." Virginia is also the productive center of *batter bread* (a soft corn cake), *lumber room* "store room," and *nicker* "whinny."

The Virginia Piedmont, the Shenandoah Valley and adjoining parts of Maryland and North Carolina have *snake doctor* "dragonfly," but the rest of the Southern area has *mosquito hawk* in this instance. Hence, in the case of the dragonfly we now have a clear division between Northern (*devil's*) *darning needle,* Midland *snake feeder,* and Southern (piedmont) *snake doctor* or (coastal) *mosquito hawk* (Map 4, p. 88).

Midland and Southern areas together, furthermore, have the terms *singletree* or *swingletree* "whiffletree," (*corn*) *pone* "corn bread," *paling/pale fence* "picket fence," *roasting ears* "sweet corn," *bucket* "pail," *spicket* "faucet," *polecat* "skunk," and *Christmas gift!* "Merry Christmas!"

In the Midland and Southern areas the word *till* is used instead of *to* in the expression "quarter *to* eleven." Here the Scottish form is supported by the general translation of German *bis* "until." Other areas of the East Coast have both *to* and *of*, with *of* more predominant in the North and *to* more frequent in the South.

Still more vocabulary differences of this kind could easily be cited. To those given by Kurath we may add some involving African loan words: *goobers* (Southern mountain) and *pinders* (South Carolina and Georgia) "peanuts," as pointed out by Raven I. McDavid, Jr., and Virginia McDavid.[3] We may also note the French loan word areas—*shivaree* (i.e., *charivari*) "wedding celebration" in northern New England, the upper Middle West, and the West generally; and *batteau* "flat-bottomed boat" around Chesapeake Bay and throughout the deep South. For the Eastern States, then, we have seen how the distribution of speech patterns has resulted from the cultural imprint of non-English peoples; namely, Dutch, German, French, and African. We will be more concerned with the contributions of these as well as of other such groups as we extend our observations of American speech westward.

[3] "Regional Linguistic Atlases in the United States," *Orbis*, V (1956), 349–386.

CHAPTER 5

# *Eastern Pronunciation*

Thus far we have paid very little attention to the matter of pronunciation. To treat the subject adequately it would be necessary for a person to become an accomplished phonetician. The International Phonetic Alphabet (IPA), which is now used in some dictionaries, would provide us with a good set of symbols. In fact, the Linguistic Atlas of the United States and Canada has used an even more precise form of scientific orthography. The Linguistic Atlas of New England, for example, exhibits an incredibly fine detail: every shade of pronunciation for each informant in every community is entered on the map itself. (See the figure on p. 7.) Unfortunately, however, such fastidious scholarship is inordinately expensive; hence there is little prospect that this form of mapping can be accomplished for the entire country. For a long time to come, therefore, New England will remain the section of the United States about which linguistic information is, in this respect, most detailed and thorough. The importance of western New England in particular for the settlement of areas still further west places the New England Atlas and derivative studies in a prominent position as valued reference material.

In our more simplified discussion here we will have to hope that standard English orthography, with all its troublesome shortcomings, can serve as a kind of phonetic notation. In this connection it is best to make one's own observations directly from the mouths of reliable speakers; the reader is encouraged to do this personally. For this purpose it may be convenient to make a list of crucial tests based on words included in the present chapter.

An essential reference work for information on Eastern pronunciation is that of Hans Kurath and Raven I. McDavid, Jr., entitled *The Pronunciation of English in the Atlantic States.*[1] In it, the basic dialect distributions outlined in Kurath's *Word Geography* have been confirmed. Two important new features of the *Pronunciation,* however, are its attention to deviating vocalic structures among cultivated speakers and its relating of linguistic data to comparable material from England. While items of pronunciation available from the latter source are scant so far, our knowledge of English speech migration will be greatly enriched when all the volumes of the *Survey of English Dialects*[2] have been published.

Beyond the Atlantic areas of the United States, only scattered reports on pronunciation exist, many of which are not scientifically thorough enough to give a broad picture of dialect differences such as is provided by vocabulary studies.[3] Like the *Word Geography,* however, *The Pronunciation of English in the Atlantic States* furnishes us with safe guideposts for examining the texture of American speech further west. Yet a number of prominent features of Eastern pronunciation are uniquely confined to coastal areas along the Atlantic and the Gulf of Mexico. One such feature, for example, is the famous "dropped *r*" mentioned above. Sections 1, 2, 6, 14, 15, 16, 17, and 18 on Map 1 are particularly involved here. In 1, 2, and 6 there is a concomitant phenomenon that is equally prevalent in British English, namely the intrusive *r* which is used as a link between vowels. Thus, something like *father-and-motha* is reversible as

[1] Ann Arbor: University of Michigan Press, 1961.

[2] Harold Orton and Eugen Dieth, *Survey of English Dialects* (Leeds: E. J. Arnold and Son, Ltd., 1962– ).

[3] A notable exception is Harold Allen's *Linguistic Atlas of the Upper Middle West* (Minneapolis: University of Minneapolis Press, 1973–75).

*mother-and-fatha,* but it is also necessary to use the "linking *r*" in *papa-r-and-máma* or *mama-r-and-papa.* Relatively few people using this system would mistakenly say *it's a good idear* but merely *it's a good idea.* They do, of course, say *the idear of it,* because the *r* is necessary in that position; and they may also be heard to say *he is sawring a boahd.* People living on the edges of such an area who neither share the system fully nor understand it, but who feel impelled to imitate it, therefore, are the real users of such phrases as *it's a good idear.*

Along with the loss of preconsonantal and final *r,* one could mention the peculiar qualities of the preceding vowels, although these would be hard to illustrate in conventional spelling. (Those who remember the voices of Franklin D. Roosevelt or John F. Kennedy will grasp the problem at once.) Suffice it to say, the vowels are generally longer, or subject to a distinct *uh*-like offglide.

We have mentioned in a previous chapter the archaic Bostonian *a* used, for example, in the shibboleth *park the car in the park;* and we can also note the retention of *r* in *car* (before the vowel of *in*). Now we may also point out the occurrence of three distinctly different vowels before *r* in Eastern coastal (not including Midland) pronunciations of *Mary, merry,* and *marry.* In the Midland and much of the West all three words are pronounced with the *e* in the first syllable of *better;* for some speakers this may apply only to words such as *Mary* and *merry,* while *marry* may have the *a* of *cat.* More widespread is the general Eastern pronunciation of *hurry* as *hah-ree* or *huh-ree,* which Westerners find alien or peculiar.

Another Eastern and Southern feature (1–6, 9–18) is the distinction between *o* and *ou/oa* in the pairs *morning–mourning, horse-hoarse.* Because early grammarians whose native habitat was somewhere within these regions felt that failure to distinguish such forms phonetically was barbarous and boorish, school books have long attempted to adopt the distinction as a presumptuous urge to elegance. Although some Western areas come by the distinction naturally—through speech migration

—others find it a ludicrous burden, and even those people who manage to make the distinction artificially are apt to err and do it in reverse.

A similar difficulty due to fancied elegance is produced by the once widespread imitation, especially among the stage-bitten, of the (waning) inland Northern, Southern, and south Midland pronunciations *tyuzday, dyou,* and *nyou* for "Tuesday," "dew," and "new." More often than not the hapless imitator will systematically transfer the cherished *y* sound to words like *do, tool, noon,* or even *moot!*

Again the pronunciation of an *h* in words like *wheelbarrow, wharf,* and *whip,* is relatively rare in everyday American speech. On the East Coast it has been largely eliminated in Pennsylvania and New Jersey, occasionally also in various Northern sections, and more sporadically throughout the deep South. The word *whinny* is pronounced with the initial *hw* sound over a large part of the Northern and Southern areas, but since animal noises—or words describing them—often require a special phonology, this word in itself cannot be considered representative. In most of England, speakers of all classes have given up the *h* sound in *wh* words long ago, although it is common in Northern dialects, notably Scottish, and it is perhaps through the influence of early Scottish schoolteachers in this country that the archaism has so long prevailed here. All signs indicate, however, that it stands little chance of survival even through the present century.

The situation is somewhat different in the case of initial *h* in *humor* or *human:* the *h*-less form *yumor* is heard throughout the Eastern United States, although *hyumor* is not infrequent, especially in the Northern area (along with an occasional occurrence of *hoomer*). It has been suggested that spelling influence is at work with this word. Some people seem to regard *yumor* as substandard; others, to whom it is an innovation, seem to regard it as an elegant form. In the Far West people prefer the form with *h.* Its future is by no means assured, but it is strengthened functionally by the distinctions of *whose* and *ooze, Hugh's/hues* and *use* (verb), etc.

A rather striking feature which marks Northern speech at least as far west as the Mississippi River is the pronunciation of the word *greasy* (Map 10, p. 94) with an unvoiced *s* (as in *messy*), whereas the Midland and Southern regions generally have *greazy* (rhyming with *easy*). It is interesting to note that some obviously Northern speakers consciously affect the form *greazy* in the belief that it must be more respectable. Affectations of this kind often arise in compensation for a feeling of inferiority; the speaker believes a natural form *must* be "wrong," since he did not acquire it through education, so he adopts an exotic form to take its place—one he may have heard on rare occasions.

A good example of this affliction is the use of a so-called broad *a,* which was once jealously acquired by schoolteachers as a fancied mark of educational refinement. The extent of "broad *a*" among the American dialects is very restricted and, even then, quite inconsistent. The struggle for its perpetuation has been given up long ago, although it has not lost face in areas where it was once original—namely, in eastern New England and among the old gentry of the coastal South. It involves the pronunciation of an *ah* sound in *calf, half, path, dance, can't, laugh, glass, rather, pasture,* etc., as opposed to the *a* sound of *fat* that prevails in other American dialects. Overcompensation on the part of eager imitators, however, leads to strange individual lapses, such as that of making *cat* sound like *cot,* pronouncing *can* as *cahn,* or eliminating the *a* sound of *fat* entirely from one's diction in order to adopt something halfway between this sound and an *ah* sound.

Short *o* is even more restricted in eastern New England, although it appears in some words in western Pennsylvania: Thus, the New Englander is often thought to be saying something like *hum* and *rud* for "home" and "road," and some people in western Pennsylvania tell us they attended *caw-ledge.*

Many more differences in pronunciation can be pointed out. Some are confined to small localities, older generations, or rustics. Others are difficult to illustrate in conventional spelling. For example, most people who have any ear at all for dialect distinctions will be able to imitate the diphthongal deviations which so strongly mark the differences between Northern and Southern speech in general. A native of Chicago may say *high time* with an *ah-ee* in both words, while a native of Galveston may say something like *hah tahm*. In certain words like *fight, might,* or *price,* however, it is possible that both speakers will agree in using the *ah-ee* diphthong. With the diphthong *ah-oo* a similar instance may be observed: Northern and Southern speech may have *ah-oo* in *house,* but in *round* the Northerner may use *ah-oo* where the Southerner has the *a*-sound of *cat,* plus a slight *oo*-sound. This last peculiarity is shared by the Southerner with various coastal areas further north, notably one around Fall River, Massachusetts.

The diphthong thus treated is reminiscent of British cockney speech and is, indeed, closely related to it. Another feature of this kind, found particularly in New York City (where it is sometimes classed as "Brooklynese"), in Charleston, and around New Orleans, is the suggestion of something like an *oi* sound in words like *bird, heard,* and *curl.* These cities were among those maintaining close contact with London for a good while, and they bear the marks of a social class which contributed heavily to their development.

A threefold division, with many exceptions, can be found with respect to the pronunciation of vowels in words like *wash* and *Washington.* If we consider Northern as normal, with its *ah* sound, we can say that the Midland areas seem to introduce an "*r* coloring," so that *wash* sounds like *worsh;* in the Southern areas it is frequently articulated more like *woish.* As we go westward from the East Coast, however, we note that the treatment of this *ah* sound before *sh* becomes quite chaotic. In the State of Washington, where Northern pronunciations predominate, the Midland *or* sound, in this case, seems to have won out. As is customary in the case of dialect contention, of course, some people will use it as a mark of Western good-fellowship and others will avoid it as being boorish.

Conditions for two different kinds of vowels in words like *roots, coop,* and *creek* are so mixed up that it is hard to generalize about them. On the East Coast, *coop* and *hoop* usually have the *oo* sound of *boot* in the Northern area (with the exception of the larger cities) and the *oo* sound of *book* in the Midland and Southern areas. The exact opposite appears to be the case in *root*. Similarly, *creek* is more often *crick* in the Northern and Midland areas, but *creek* (rhyming with *peek*) in Southern areas. In all instances, of course, spelling influence is strong, and certain pedagogical taboos are involved. The distribution in Eastern sections, as we shall see in other examples, generally tends to prevail also in secondary settlements further west.

One of the most complicated of all differences in the pronunciation of American English is the use of *ah* as opposed to *aw* in certain types of words. All through the Northern part of the United States and in Canada, many people will find this statement meaningless, simply because they do not make a distinction between *ah* and *aw*. No stigma of inferiority should be attached to this circumstance, however, since the need to distinguish meaning by contrasting *ah* and *aw* is usually dissipated by the clarity of context. But those who do not recognize the distinction will have to listen very carefully to notice a difference like this in the usage of others, for the listener often supplies within the framework of his own speech the sound *he thinks he hears*. To be a good observer of speech differences, especially in closely related dialects, one must learn to free himself from the prejudice of his own habits.

If a speaker actually uses, consistently and noticeably, different vowel sounds in *cot–caught, hock–hawk, sot–sought, collar–caller, don–dawn,* or any such otherwise identical pair of words (with respect to pronunciation—not spelling), he will recognize what is meant by the *ah–aw* contrast, and it is probable that his speech contains one vowel more than that of some of his neighbors. Yet the two sounds may still be utilized in the speech of a given person without any such contrast actually occurring. Some people, for example, have *ah* in all the words just listed, but *aw* before *l* in *call, salt,* and *bald,* before *f* in *soft, off,* and *cough,* before *s* in *loss, toss,* and *frost,* before *n* or *ng* in *on, lawn, long,* and *laundry,* or before *g* in *log, dog, fog,* and *hog.* The various combinations are manifold; one and the same person may say *lawg* and *fahg,* with contrasting vowels. What is even more bewildering is the fact that the distinction tends to vanish in rapid speech; or it may even be optional. People who habitually distinguish *ah* from *aw* sometimes react visibly to the failure of others to do so, either by smiling or by asking for clarification.

In his book, *An Introduction to the Phonetics of American English,*[3] C. K. Thomas, of Cornell University, has attempted to suggest some regional tendencies among the dialect areas of the Eastern United States; *lahg* "log," *mahk* "mock," *lahng* "long," and *hahnk* "honk," he contends, are common on the East Coast from Boston to Philadelphia; otherwise *lawg, mawk, lawng,* and *hawnk* prevail; *ahn* "on" is general in the North, but southward from southern New Jersey and southeastern Pennsylvania, as well as to the west, *awn* is current.

Regarding the variation of *ah–aw* before *r,* the words *forest, orange, horrible, correspond,* and *moral* have an *ah* sound in the speech of the New England Coast, New York City, the Atlantic Coast, and the inland South. Oregonians recognize an outlander from such places by his pronunciation, *ahregon* "Oregon" instead of *ohregon* or *awregon.*

Finally, in our survey of Eastern pronunciation, we should note once more the treatment of words like *hurry,* which are pronounced with *uh* (*huh-ree*) along the Atlantic seaboard and in the inland South; everywhere else, including the West, an "American *r*" is used (*her-ee*).

[3] 2nd ed. (New York: Ronald Press, 1958).

CHAPTER 6

# Eastern Grammar

While it is possible to comprehend the entire range of a given speaker's pronunciation by studying fairly small samples of his language, grammatical details are harder to organize. A complete study of grammar would require a much longer text than can be included economically in an Atlas questionnaire. Furthermore, it is particularly the grammatical aspects of language that receive the greatest attention in our schools, so that regional differences are complicated in proportion to the amount and type of formal educational influence in given areas. Among the various forms to be treated here, folk speech will provide most of the clues to regional patterns; but we shall be able to assess to a limited extent also the manner in which the everyday usage of educated persons is involved.

From the files of the Linguistic Atlas, the late E. B. Atwood, of the University of Texas, assembled information of this kind in his book, *A Survey of Verb Forms in the Eastern United States.*[1] This book presents charts for the distribution of expressions like *I axed him, he was dogbit, who catched it, I have clum, he drug a log, I holp myself,* and *he drawed it out.* These will sound quaint to the average Westerner, although he may readily

[1] Ann Arbor: University of Michigan Press, 1953.

accept such phrases as *he laid in bed, he seen me, who rung the bell, he was hung, he done it,* and *here's your clothes.* Even the most highly educated people have difficulty deciding on the "correct" form of the following: *I dreamt/dreamed all night; she knelt/kneeled; they knit/knitted the sweaters; he pled/pleaded guilty; the collar shrank/shrunk;* and *he dove/dived in.* Those whose reading has made them familiar with the literature of past centuries, or with British writing, may turn out to be more conservative in this respect than people whose principal reading material is the newspaper or the farmer's almanac.

As far as "correctness" is concerned, we know this is a matter that is generally determined more by usage than by prescription. In this sense all grammatical changes may be regarded as legitimized errors. A "regular" pattern is often the strongest, so that we may feel more comfortable in using *cleaved,* rather than *clove* or *cleft,* as the past tense form of *cleave;* or we may accept *has he showed up yet?* and balk at *they've shown him up.* Yet the expressions *have growed* and *have blowed* are held beyond the pale. The regularizing of "irregular" verbs, however, has a long and honorable history which may be observed even in the earliest English literature. It is no wonder, therefore, that different levels of speech and various migrating groups of speakers should bear the marks of such historical transition.

Folk speech of the areas where the first colonies were established frequently has a past-tense form of *see* which is the same as that of the present tense. From New England this usage extends westward toward the Great Lakes, though in tidewater Virginia and in South Carolina it is more restricted. *Seen,* as past tense, is common everywhere but especially in the Midland areas, while *seed* is strictly south Midland and Southern. Map 11 (p. 95) (*he seed me*) combines the information given by Atwood with that furnished by the McDavids in the article cited. The expression *dogbit* "bitten by a dog" has roughly the same distribution.

Another example of this type is given in Map 12, (p. 96), where the Northern variant *hadn't ought to* is opposed to Midland and Southern *oughtn't* (although *hadn't ought to* is also found in coastal North Carolina).

A clearly Northern form is the word *dove* "dived," which seems to be gaining ground in the West, even among cultured speakers who have long suffered the fears of academic censure.[2] An archaism, *div,* is used occasionally in northeastern New England and the coastal and mountain areas of the South and South Midland. In southern New Jersey rare occurrences of *duv* are also encountered.

All through the back country of the Eastern States, isolated instances of *ett* for *ate* are heard. (This is more a matter of pronunciation than of grammar, of course.) British English employs this pronunciation almost exclusively; in England *ate* is a provincialism (the past tense is spelled *eat,* pronounced *ett*), and in the United States *ett* is an archaism. If we recall the Shakespearean and Biblical verb forms, *blowed, growed, shrinked,* and *holp,* it will be obvious to us that American English has accepted some innovations of that time and rejected others. The occurrence of such forms among more isolated and older people of the Eastern mountain areas may be identified very often as understandable archaism rather than mere perversity or wrongheadedness.

The persistence of grammatical diversity among the dialects continues to be reflected in Western speech. In the following chapters we will be concerned with grammatical trace-forms, even though information about them is largely overshadowed by vocabulary studies. The reason for this is clear: Grammatical forms can only be tested efficiently through personal interviews; postal sampling permits too much time for reflection and self-correction. In our educational system, it is grammar that is most subject to correction or censure, and literary responses tend to depart from colloquial reality.

[2] A number of prominent writers, such as Ernest Hemingway, have used and thus contributed to the literary prestige of *dove.*

CHAPTER 7

# The Westward Movement

The coastal and mountain areas studied in the preceding chapters have remained reasonably stable for a long period of time. During the latter part of the eighteenth century, particularly after the Revolution, people began to push westward. By 1850 these pioneers had reached the ninety-fifth meridian and were in the process of continuing on to the Pacific Coast without pausing to settle the intervening wilderness.

The earliest westward movement beyond the Appalachian Range was directed toward the Ohio Valley. Principal contributors to the influx of population there were the Yankee farmers living in the western part of New England, the frontiersmen from the Midlands, and the backwoods people of the upland South. While it is true that population movement in the United States has always tended to follow the lines of latitude from east to west, there was an appreciable scattering and mixing of Eastern people among the Western settlements, so that lines of dialect difference have only gradually begun to make themselves evident in the Middle West and scarcely at all in the Far West. Fewer distinctions coincide with one another, and isogloss bands have to be treated as successive waves in the transition from one core-area to another. In many instances we can speak only of "dominant" or "shared" features, where dialect forms originating in different areas are commingled and have become interchangeable. Occasionally we have to do with cases of semantic specialization, both local and extended. The Northern term *pail,* for example, comes into conflict with the Midland term *bucket,* and we are told that *pail* "does not mean the same thing"—opinions about the exact difference will vary, even from family to family. The same is true for *dragonfly* and a number of other terms in which this phenomenon (called "secondary semantic differentiation") is observed.

Settlement of the Ohio Valley began in two ways—through the establishment of "land" companies and through individual parceling in "reserve" areas, principally to war veterans, who were thus finally paid for their services to their country. A section of land south of Lake Erie, called the Western Reserve, was established in 1786 for the benefit of settlers from Connecticut, and Ohio Company lands were settled by people from western Massachusetts in 1788. An area around present-day Marietta was taken up shortly thereafter by people from the western parts of the Middle Atlantic States, including Virginia. Kentucky and New Jersey people joined in establishing themselves between Cincinnati and Dayton in 1790. Virginians and Marylanders received grants in the Virginia Military District (between Manchester and Columbus) in 1795. Germans and Scotch-Irish from Pennsylvania soon augmented these various groups, thus further complicating the checkerboard resettlement of Eastern people.

As these groups expanded and more land was needed, a concerted process of inner migration—in longer and longer stretches—got under way. It has been noted that New Englanders generally planned their migrations in such a way that they could move in a body to a given section of land; but Midlanders and Southerners, as typical frontiersmen, were satisfied to take up land at various places in small parcels, so that unless they succeeded in filling a gap for an extended period of time, they stood a good chance of losing their identity among their Yankee neighbors.

Midlanders and Southerners followed the course of rivers westward and entered Ohio, Indiana, and Illinois by way of the Miami, Wabash, Kaskaskia, and Illinois Rivers. Northerners followed the Great Lakes, which they reached by way of the Mohawk Valley. In anticipation of a war with Great Britain and the subsequent need of agrarian support, various western roads and canals were projected and eventually built. The National or Cumberland Road (1811), the Erie Canal (1825), the Forbes Road through the mountains of Pennsylvania, and the Wilderness Road through the Virginia mountains especially accelerated the Ohio Valley settlements.

Farming in the Great Lakes region was of a diversified character, with grain the most widely produced item. Southern areas, including western Georgia, northern Alabama, and Mississippi, now became a huge cotton-producing section. Eli Whitney invented the cotton gin in 1793, and the demand for cotton land began to grow, so that a rapid westward movement followed the southern spurs of the Appalachian Range and soon extended through the entire American territory along the Gulf of Mexico. The institution of slavery grew accordingly, and when the importation of slaves was finally stopped, slave husbandry became the principal industry of the upper Southern states.[1] Agriculturally, the South now became a two-product region, with tobacco and cotton reigning supreme. It is easy to imagine, therefore, that the dialects established there should have been more unified among themselves than those of the North. But at the same time, the unique economic patterns of the South were instrumental in establishing class levels that have been reflected in the English spoken there even to the present day. The traditional rapport between Southern planters and English manufacturers was to be accentuated later on by

[1] William Miller, *A History of the United States* (New York: Dell Publishing Co., 1958), p. 184.

the divisions of North and South over the slave question, and this struggle in itself, as we shall see, was responsible for a cleavage that had noticeable aftereffects in the settlement of the Far West.

CHAPTER 8

# Sectional Atlas Studies

## *The Great Lakes Area*

In his unpublished dissertation "A Word Atlas of the Great Lakes Region,"[1] A. L. Davis has given an excellent account of American dialects as they can be identified through vocabulary in Ohio, Indiana, Illinois, and Michigan. The details of settlement history are here related to dialect consequences. Thus, the materials presented by Kurath for the Eastern States can be articulated now with their Western offshoots.

In Davis's work we have the advantage of being able to observe the manner in which language grows and changes as the result of dialect mixture. The usual door-to-door technique of Atlas recording, furthermore, is here given added validity by the use of supplementary mail questionnaires, so that a greater saturation of area has been possible than might have been financially feasible with conventional methods. As we may well surmise from our observations of settlement in the Great Lakes area, the complex intermingling of transitional areas can be studied in fine detail only with the aid of a statistical treatment of known dialect variants. Accordingly, a kind of calculus has been devised by linguists to deal with such transitional distribu-

[1] Doctoral dissertation, University of Michigan, 1948.

tion as well as with the relative frequency of deviation from place to place. Such a technique becomes increasingly necessary in newer, geographically more complicated areas such as the Pacific Northwest.

Map 15 (p. 99) gives a general threefold division suggested by Davis's material. While Area I corresponds to the completely "Northern" dialect area of Map 1, Areas II and III are actually divisions of various Midland characteristics. Strictly "Southern" features play no appreciable role in the Great Lakes Area. Thus, the three areas may be illustrated in the gradual north-to-south orientation of the words *pail* and *bucket:* I. *pail;* II. *pail* or *bucket;* III. *bucket.*

Considered in another way, Area I is set apart by the average northern limits of Midland forms, and Area III by the average southern limits of Northern forms. The provenience of such forms is usually predicated on the basis of material given in Kurath's *Word Geography,* but circumstances of topography and settlement history have combined to complicate the perspective here.

Maps 14–17 (pp. 98–101) illustrate various isogloss bundles showing particularly the strong continuation of Northern versus Midland areas, corresponding to Davis's projection of Area I in Map 13. These isoglosses are restrictive rather than privative; that is, they generally show the northern limits of Midland terms, even though these occur alongside certain other (including Northern) terms.

Thus, Map 14 shows the northern limits of the Midland *quarter till eleven, corn shuck, barn* (*cow, feed*) *lot, sick at the stomach,* and *corn pone. Quarter till* occurs in competition with, and alongside of, the Northern *quarter to* or *quarter of;* in the Eastern states, *to* and *of* are common in the Northern area, with *to* also frequent in Delmarva. *Of* predominates in Ohio, *to* in Michigan. South Midland and Southern *corn shuck* is opposed to Northern and North Midland *corn husk* (Area I), although the latter also occurs in central Ohio, Indiana, and Illinois. *Barnyard* is general Northern; forms with *lot* are South Midland

and Southern (compare the correspondingly more restricted distribution here with that of *pulley bone* on Map 16, or of *light bread* of Map 17, both of which suffer limitations of provenience). While *sick to the stomach* is the common Northern expression, and *sick at the stomach* is found in the Midland and Southern areas, the latter is also current in southern New England and around New York City. *Corn pone* is again Midland and Southern, in contrast to the widespread Northern term, *johnny cake*.

Map 15 is given to show the overlapping of two core-areas: the northern limits of Midland *sook!* (a call to cows) and the southern limits of the synonymous *co boss*(*ie*) are thus seen to overlap more extensively as they go westward.

Map 16 indicates a fairly stable agreement with regard to the northern limits of Midland *smearcase, shafts,* and *dog irons/fire dogs;* included here too are the more southern isoglosses for Midland and Southern *pulley bone* and *cherry seed* (against Northern *wishbone* and *cherry pit,* respectively). *Smearcase,* competing with Northern *Dutch cheese,* alternates with *curds* or *cruds* along the Ohio River (a relic form used occasionally in eastern Pennsylvania and in the Kanawha Valley of West Virginia) and with south Midland and Southern *clabber*(*ed*)/*clobber*(*ed*) *cheese* in Ohio and Indiana. *Shafts* opposes Northern *fills/thills,* and roughly parallels lines which could be given for Midland and Southern *singletree/swingletree* versus Northern *whiffletree/whippletree,* as well as for Midland *nicker* versus Northern *whinny* (see Map 9, p. 93). *Dog irons* is in contrast to Northern *andirons* along the line given, but occurs interchangeably with it south of the line; *fire dogs* occurs sporadically in Ohio and Indiana.

Map 17 combines three isoglosses which extend to the north of the Indiana border into Michigan, encompassing all of Indiana. This accentuates a tendency seen on some of the preceding maps. Included here are the North Midland *snake feeder,* Midland *nicker,* and South Midland and Midland *light bread.* Opposed to these are the corresponding Northern terms, *darn-*

*ing needle, whinny,* and *white bread.* The Southern piedmont term, *snake doctor,* is used here and there, while Southern coastal *mosquito hawk* occurs but rarely.

Indications are that features of pronunciation and grammar in the Great Lakes area will have the same distribution as the vocabulary. Maps 9–12 reveal this to some degree. The late Professor A. H. Marckwardt, formerly of the University of Michigan, later at Princeton University, published some material that further substantiates this claim. His article "Principal and Subsidiary Dialect Areas in the North-Central States"[2] gives a more detailed description of the settlement history and a few more illustrations than we have provided here. The *greasy–greazy* line (Map 10) has been mentioned in our preceding discussion, and Marckwardt wrote a good deal on the complicated question of *ah–aw* differences, which we have also mentioned earlier.

With the key words *foggy* and *hog,* Marckwardt (see the Bibliography) finds *aw* regularly in Ohio, usually in Indiana, and frequently in Illinois; *ah* is used all through Michigan and in the Chicago area of Illinois. In *swamp, war, warmed, wash, washing, Washington,* and *wasp, ah* is more frequent in Michigan, Indiana, and southeastern Wisconsin; otherwise *aw* prevails. The same is true for *swallow, want,* and *water.*

A more complicated situation exists for the pronunciation of the stressed syllable in *borrow* and *tomorrow,* which can have the vowel sound of *ore* or of *are;* the *ore* type, which predominates in northern and western Ohio and most of Indiana, occurs sporadically in Michigan and occasionally in Illinois (including Chicago); the *are* type is frequent all along the Ohio River, in central and northwestern Illinois, and in Michigan generally.

Publications on other dialect features in this area are few and far between. At the annual meetings of the Modern Lan-

[2] *Publication of the American Dialect Society,* No. 27 (April, 1957), pp. 3–15.

guage Association in 1957, Virginia McDavid spoke on the grammatical forms of the North-Central States. Her examples were mainly from substandard speech, and many of the expressions listed seem to be rare or receding. In addition to those noted in Maps 9–12 here, she mentioned such forms as *he driv, riz, div, clim, ketcht,* and *it shrinkt* among those in local usage; *dove* is a prevalent form, and both *I seen* and *he clum* appear to be on the increase. Eastern Kentucky still has forms like *het* "heated," *drimpt* "dreamed," *them there, scairt, I might could,* etc. In quaint or uneducated speech in general she finds *I growed, throwed, blowed, come, run, drownded,* also *a-singin', hain't/ain't, we/you was, he don't care, have drank,* etc. Even among the educated, *I been thinkin', like I said,* and *he laid around* are common enough, and *it's me* is almost universal.[3]

Besides the area illustrated in Maps 13–17, Wisconsin, Kentucky, and part of southern Ontario are included in the Atlas of the North-Central States. F. G. Cassidy, of the University of Wisconsin, has done a good deal of research in Wisconsin, some results of which are summarized in an article entitled "Some New England Words in Wisconsin."[4] Here he deals with the so-called Yankee element. His investigation shows that New England has had a strong influence on the vocabulary used in Wisconsin. But he points out the fact that older forms, such as *Dutch cheese* and *stoop,* are everywhere on the wane. He thus demonstrates the inroads made by the term *cottage cheese* upon Eastern folk terms that we have mentioned above: *smearcase* seems to be supported by the large German immigrant population of the state; yet in general, as Cassidy says, "the foreign-derived population has apparently adopted the current local American lexical pattern with insignificant variations" (p. 339). The only meaningful distribution among Cassidy's examples is

[3] See: R. I. McDavid, Jr., and V. G. McDavid. "Grammatical Differences in the North Central States," *American Speech,* XXXV (Feb., 1960), 5–19.

[4] *Language,* XVII (Oct.–Dec., 1941), 324–339.

the one given for (Midland) *nicker,* which occurs regularly along the southern border of the state. A similar restriction with regard to *belly-bump* "face down on a sled" is more problematical; while this term is common in Pennsylvania (hence "North Midland" in this respect), it is also very frequent in eastern New England. The more familiar Midland term, *belly-buster,* is apparently little known in Wisconsin.

## *The Upper Middle West*

*The Linguistic Atlas of the Upper Midwest* is now available in two volumes. The work is directed by H. B. Allen, of the University of Minnesota, who supervised Virginia McDavid's thesis "Verb Forms in the North-Central States and the Upper Midwest."[5] In "The Linguistic Atlas of the Upper Midwest of the United States,"[6] Allen shows the isogloss for Northern *belly-flop* "face down on a sled" and Midland *belly-buster* continuing across northern Iowa, then up along the Missouri River as far as Pierre, S.D., and then in a northwesterly direction towards the southern border of Montana. The relative incidence of Northern and Midland terms in this entire area, however, leads him to the conclusion that "the Midland dialect is expanding and the Northern is contracting west of the Mississippi" (p. 94).

Thus he particularly emphasizes the unique conditions of the growing West: sudden rise of cities after the coming of the railroads, primary influx of foreign-born groups, and economic or geographical factors giving rise to new adaptations of linguistic usage. The term *belly-buster* has at least twenty variants of known provenience in this area, but there are also numerous innovations, and the same situation is to be expected for other items. The term *belly-slam* or *slamming* for the same activity begins in this area and is carried westward into the Rocky

[5] Doctoral dissertation, University of Minnesota, 1957.
[6] *Orbis,* I (1952), 89–94; and LAUM, p. 390f.

Mountains.[7] Conversely, Western mountain and range terms extend eastward into this area.

The Upper Midwest is then a crossroads joining the traditions of the East to the conditions of the growing West. Dialect mixture is active, and speech innovation is the order of the day. Over eighty different terms, for example, are used as rough-and-ready designation for rural dwellers, and some of these terms show definite regional distribution; others seem to be the ad hoc response to a poetic urge. A few listed by Allen are *sod-buster/soddy, hayshaker, honyock(er), hillbilly,* and *jackpine/cedar savage, bushwhacker, shacker, rabbit-choker, jackfish farmer,* and *sandhiller.*

## *Texas*

For a number of years, the late E. B. Atwood, of the University of Texas, was engaged in making (written) records of Texas vocabulary. He described the work in an article entitled "A Preliminary Report on Texas Word Geography"[8] and in a paper read at the summer meetings of the Linguistic Society of America in 1958.

Here he indicated that Texas word geography would probably reveal no clear isoglosses, but rather a kind of statistical dispersion. Although many items in his book *The Regional Vocabulary of Texas,*[9] published in 1962, bore out his earlier predictions, certain definite patterns could still be discerned. Texas vocabulary in general is predominantly Midland and Southern, with purely Southern terms in the minority.

Western Texas has a lower incidence of Southern words than eastern Texas, and in the opinion of people who have studied the matter from admittedly scant information, pronunciation

[7] While no one has previously recorded this expression from areas further east, Joseph Friend, of Southern Illinois University, reports having heard it used as the common expression when he was a boy in Toledo, Ohio (c. 1917–1921).

[8] *Orbis,* II (1953), 61–66.

[9] Austin: The University of Texas Press, 1962.

follows the same pattern. "Eastern Texas," says Atwood, "is somewhat more 'Southern,' but not strikingly so." According to his figures, moreover, northern Texas has the highest relative number of South Midland and Southern terms.

In Texas as a whole, the South Midland and Southern terms *sook!* (call to cows), *French harp* "harmonica," (*barn*) *lot* "barnyard," *you-all* "you" (pl.), *Christmas gift!* "Merry Christmas!" (*corn*) *shucks, light bread* "wheat bread," *pulley bone* "wishbone," and *tow sack* "burlap bag" are most prevalent; and the Southern terms, *carry* "to escort," *snap beans* "green beans," *chitlins* "fried intestines of swine," *tote* "to carry," *croker sack* "burlap bag," and *low* "to moo" are strongly represented.

The commercial term *cottage cheese* is now quite common, *smearcase* is associated with German settlements, and the South Midland and Southern *clabber cheese* ranges in frequency from 7 per cent in southern Texas to 40 per cent in northern Texas. A South Midland and Southern word, *branch* "creek," is common but restricted to areas in which the item itself is found. The "Western" word *corral* seems to be on the increase, at the expense of *lot* and *barnyard;* and South Midland–Southern *green beans* competes vigorously with Southern *snap beans.*

Texas is uniquely situated with respect to foreign culture, with Louisiana French making inroads on the eastern border and Mexican Spanish entering along the southern border. Thus, from Louisiana, Texas has the terms *jambalaya* "rice stew," *bayou* "inlet," *banquette* "sidewalk," and *lagniappe* "extra gift with a purchase"; and from the Spanish, *mesa* "dry plateau," *mott* "clump of trees," *lariat* "rope with a noose," *chaparral* "thicket," *arroyo* "dry creek bed," *hackamore* "rope halter," *pilon* "extra gift with a purchase" (cf. *lagniappe* above), and others.

In an intensive study of several counties, entitled "A Southeast Texas Dialect Study"[10] A. M. Z. Norman, then of Louisiana

[10] *Orbis,* V (1956), 61–79.

State University, later at the University of Texas, tested the incidence of words listed in Kurath's *Word Geography,* with the following results: Northern terms—11.8 per cent; exclusively Midland terms—28.5 per cent; combined South Midland and Southern terms—54.5 per cent.

Norman also commented briefly on the pronunciation of the area studied, summarizing thus: the sounds *hw-* and *hy-* are used in words like *white* and *humor; ty-, dy-,* and *ny-* occur regularly in *tube, due, new,* etc.; *borrow, Florida, orange, fog,* and *foggy* have the sound *aw,* not *ah;* words like *class* have a diphthongal off-glide (result: something like *cla-iss*); words like *chances* have a distinct *-iz* ending; and the pairs *card–cord, bar–bore, car–core, tar–tore,* etc. sound alike.

Studies of settlement history in Texas would lead one to expect a more distinctly "Southern" dialect in the eastern part of the state, and a definitely Midland, particularly Southern-mountain type in the northern and western parts of the state. Pronunciation, as far as it has been observed, would seem to bear this out, but vocabulary seems to have fused quite rapidly in the direction of more northerly elements. The general mixture of competing terms here, however, is no novelty, as we shall see from subsequent observation of other Western states.

## *Colorado*

The key to a linguistic geography of the Rocky Mountain area is Colorado, where Atlas work was completed by an energetic scholar, Marjorie Kimmerle, of the University of Colorado. In collaboration with the McDavids, she published an article in 1951 entitled "Problems of Linguistic Geography in the Rocky Mountain Area."[11] Map 18 (p. 102) illustrates some of the information given there.

If one proceeds cautiously, he will discern the possibility of an isogloss for the now-familiar *greasy–greazy* line, which di-

[11] *The Western Humanities Review,* V (1951), 249–264.

vides Northern and Midland areas generally. Likewise, Northern *Dutch cheese* contrasts with *clabber cheese,* and at least the southeastern section of the state reveals an incidence of *French harp,* which was found to be the regular form in Texas. Among the nonstandard forms for "climbed" we note here the Northern *clim* along the northern border; beyond this the Southern *clum* is heard. Thus, Colorado seems to be a natural dividing point for certain identifiable Northern and Midland words—distributed correspondingly in the northern and southern parts of the state.

As in Texas, a number of isoglosses for items of vocabulary were found to run north and south through the center of the state. In his *Colorado Word Geography,*[12] Clyde T. Hankey, of Youngstown University, illustrates the overlapping borders of coincidence of the term *prairie dog* (with a western limit running north and south in the mountain regions) and *park* "mountain meadow" (whose eastern limit runs the same way). Hankey's isoglosses are generally too spotty to indicate a clear extension of Eastern terms, but he deserves the credit for having analyzed also some important social features of vocabulary distribution. "In Colorado," he says, "these social differences are often the most easily observable conditions of distribution . . ." (p. 56). In older folk-speech, for example, one sometimes hears the expression *sick in the stomach;* more commonly, however, it is *sick to the stomach,* whereas in cultivated speech it is *sick at the stomach.*

Again as in Texas, Spanish influence is especially noticeable: *corral, ranch, canyon, adobe, chaps* are widespread. Their remarkable spread from Southwestern states is clear testimony for common economic interests throughout the Rocky Mountain area.

Pronunciation seems to follow similar patterns; in Map 18 (p. 102) we may note the Northern use of the *oo* sound of *book* (designated [ʊ]) attested for words like *roof* and *root,* in con-

[12] *Publication of the American Dialect Society,* No. 34 (Nov., 1960).

trast with a more Southern use of the *oo* sound of *boot* in similar words.

Because of the isolated nature of individual settlements, entire towns have sprung up in Colorado (as, of course, everywhere in the Rockies) without benefit of intervening agriculture. Some have flourished for a while and been abandoned—or enjoyed a rebirth. Such tenuous existence must surely have had its effect upon the population distribution and, with it, upon various dialect ingredients. Indeed, it is surprising that any patterns at all should manifest themselves. As always, however, means of access prove to be the determining factors, so that along with the general westward movement, the principal river valleys point out both the origin and the destination of many incoming settlers.

## *Other Rocky Mountain Areas: Northern and Southern Sections*

Divisions suggested by key words given for Colorado do not preclude extensive intermixture in other instances either to the north or to the south. In describing the speech of Wyoming, for example, W. O. Clough says:

"The original speech pattern would seem to have been laid down by New York, New England, Pennsylvania and Ohio, that is, largely the New England speech area, plus a mixture of northern Midland. The foreign population, heavily British, would in some degree reinforce that pattern; and the sprinkling from Missouri, and the smaller number from Virginia, West Virginia, Kentucky, and Maryland, would not greatly modify it. The northeastern dominance, however, was destined to give way to Midland pressures, though a few traces may linger today."[13]

The use of *quarter of/to/till,* Clough says, is about equal in Laramie; *to* is dominant in western, especially southwestern Wyoming; *to* and *till* compete in the middle of the state; and *of*

[13] "Some Wyoming Speech Patterns," *American Speech,* XXIX (Feb., 1954), 29.

is preferred in the urban centers. The Midland terms *coal oil* and *roasting-ears* occur in eastern and southeastern Wyoming and *hayshock* in the western part of the state. *Gunny sack* and *angleworm* are common everywhere, as is Northern *whinny*. Western *corral* predominates; *broncbuster* alternates with *wrangler* (or *broomtail* in southern Wyoming); *cowboy* and *cowpuncher* are generally favored (but *cowpoke* predominates in southeastern Wyoming).

This constitutes most of the information currently available on Wyoming. Even less is known about Montana, although mail questionnaires for the entire state have been projected, and some field work has been done.[14] Eastern Montana may be regarded generally as an extension of the Dakotas, as far as the dialects are concerned. In the southwestern section a large Missouri element is represented, in which chiefly Midland speech may be expected to appear. Northern Montana may turn out to be a Northern–Midland mixture, as is western Montana, records of which are available in the Linguistic Atlas of the Pacific Northwest, and part of which—with adjacent Idaho—once belonged to the Oregon Territory.

In other states bordering Colorado, field work has gone on apace, but publications are scanty so far. John McKendrick, of Brigham Young University, has been studying Utah; and T. M. Pearce, of the University of New Mexico, has done a good deal of work in his state. From various data reported by these scholars, it is evident that the geographical distribution of dialect features in Utah and New Mexico is exceedingly complex. (So far, no systematic information is available from Arizona.)

While Colorado shares Northern and Midland terms on a geographic basis, as illustrated in Map 18, Utah generally shows a preference for Northern terms, although the southern part of the state sometimes participates in Midland usage. Northern terms as such are relatively rare in New Mexico, where a num-

[14] Thomas J. O'Hare, "The Linguistic Geography of Eastern Montana." Doctoral dissertation, University of Texas, 1964; microfilm.

ber of words known chiefly to inhabitants of Eastern coastal areas seem to have been circulated.

Thus, Utah and Colorado usually have the Northern terms *teeter-totter/teeter (board), johnny cake, Dutch cheese, angleworm,* and *sick to the stomach,* while New Mexico has *seesaw* (as a folk term, current in the South), *batter bread/spoon bread/cracklin bread* (Chesapeake Bay and other tidewater areas), *curds* (ditto), *earthworm* (same as for *seesaw*), and *sick at the stomach* (South Midland plus New York City, Connecticut, and Rhode Island).

Utah, New Mexico, and Colorado all have the Northern (and Chesapeake Bay) term *angleworm.* Utah and Colorado share the Midland and Southern nonstandard form *clum* "climbed." Colorado and New Mexico share Midland and South Midland *belly-buster* "face down on a sled," Northern and Midland *fishworm,* Midland *smearcase,* and, occasionally, South Midland and Southern *clabber cheese.*

The crossbreeding of vocabulary types is thus a matter of development within the area after the primary influx of settlers. The high number of odd variants, especially in New Mexico, reflects the relative isolation of individual communities in an area which has developed rather recently, and in which population is still relatively sparse.

During the last twenty years the Rocky Mountain states have experienced a steady increase in population, a large part of which derives from the Pacific Coast. For in the development of the West, migration has proceeded generally nonstop between the Middle West and the Far West. But the new resources in water power, irrigation, and metals—as well as more efficient means of transportation—have made desert and mountain areas both valuable and attractive. Whatever the future holds for American dialects, observations made for the speech of this area are extremely tentative and time-bound. In view of the present movement from the Pacific Coast inland, we may well expect a significant change in cultural and economic patterns. We should, therefore, regard the speech of the Pacific Coast from the twofold aspect of internal growth and external extension.

## *California*

In California, which is now the most rapidly growing state in the Union as far as population and economic development are concerned, it was essential that Atlas work be done quickly to have any kind of validity. Fortunately, David Reed and his co-workers at the University of California were able to make records throughout the state in less than ten years' time—assisted substantially by financial aid from a wise and far-seeing state government.

In spite of a rapid increase in population, dialect conditions in California are less tenuous than in the Western mountain states because of the establishment of large urban centers and contiguous agricultural areas. Part of the settlement, as we know, was overland, and part by sea. San Francisco, for example, maintains a class dialect to this day which is strongly reminiscent of Bostonese, even though the vast majority of the people there use a typical Northern–Midland type of speech such as one might encounter in Illinois, Iowa, or northern Colorado. The large contingents of Spanish-Americans and Chinese who have lived in California for generations serve, by their presence, as a stabilizing influence, since their English tends to preserve the characteristics afforded by early settlement.

California settlement history itself indicates that natives of the northern Atlantic Coast and the upper Midwestern states have generally outnumbered those from other regions over a long period of time. It is logical to assume, therefore, that whenever variant elements of American dialects are involved, this fact will be reflected in the speech of Californians. The principal land routes of western migration began in Missouri and Iowa and continued along a common path until their point of division at the Rocky Mountains, where they went their respective ways to the North, on the Oregon Trail, and to the South, following the California Trail and the Mormon Trail. Other routes, such as that of the Butterfield Overland Mail, brought settlers into southern California. But a lively intermingling has since taken place, stimulated by various mineral discoveries and the ease of water transportation. Although some of the human ingredients of both Oregon and California were of the same mold, each area also has had its unique additions; more northerly elements gained ascendency in the Oregon Territory, and some southern elements made their way into California. Political events, especially the slavery issue, also exercised control here.

It turns out, however, that the establishment of isoglosses in the Pacific Coast states is either impractical or impossible. The best that can be done at present to quantify the information obtained from records here is to present statistical tables indicating the relative frequency of linguistic forms having a known provenience. In addition we may note certain innovations. By establishing a kind of "participation rate" among such forms in various places (keeping in mind the different social levels and all the economic factors involved), we can observe the way in which dialects of these areas have grown, and perhaps we can guess what the future will have in store for them.

Information of this kind for California was thus assembled by David Reed in an article entitled "Eastern Dialect Words in California."[15] Because of the interesting relationship between this material and that compiled from the Pacific Northwest, we will postpone an examination of it until the next section of this chapter.

## *The Pacific Northwest*

Because of the peculiar history of the old Oregon Country, and the even more unique conditions in the subsequent Wash-

[15] *Publication of the American Dialect Society,* No. 21 (April, 1954), pp. 3–15.

ington Territory, the Pacific Northwest states cannot be regarded as a mere monolithic extension of northern California. (David Reed, for example, predicted that the word *chesterfield* "sofa," occurring frequently in northern California, would be current in Oregon and Washington, but this proved to be true for only a single county of southwestern Oregon). The proportional make-up of early settlements in the Northwest, however, would give us no reason to conclude otherwise. The movement of people from East to West during the nineteenth century, as we have noted, proceeded generally in a parallel manner, so that the Oregon Country (including the present states of Oregon, Washington, and Idaho, as well as a small part of western Montana) was populated largely by Northern and Midland groups.

Until the settlement of boundary questions between Great Britain and the United States in 1846, the present Washington area west and north of the Columbia River received very few settlers, while the new population spread out rapidly in the Willamette Valley, penetrating at first only as far as navigable water permitted and maintaining close ties as a matter of mutual protection. The creation of a separate Washington Territory in 1853 coincided with a sudden increase of population around the shores of Puget Sound. Newcomers arriving by way of the Snake and Columbia Rivers moved southward along the Willamette, northward by way of the Cowlitz, or westward to the lower Columbia. Oregon had a comparatively flourishing population long before any appreciable settlement was made in the area which is now Washington. The largest infusion of settlers here in those early days was from Missouri, although Illinois and Iowa also contributed heavily to their number. Californians were especially dominant in the southernmost counties of Oregon and—along with New Yorkers—were well represented in the larger cities.

From the census figures of 1880 it may be noted that the Missouri element continued to predominate in Oregon, but that people from more northerly areas had already gained the majority in Washington. Washington has long since matched Oregon in population and economic potential, and the commercial rivalry which manifested itself between the two states as early as 1853 has been accentuated throughout the years by a competitive struggle between the interests of the Willamette Valley and those of the Puget Sound country. The symbols of this struggle are plainly visible in any historical atlas which depicts the course of early wagon roads from the Middle Western areas (known to people on the Pacific Coast as the "East") or the subsequent railroad lines and U.S. highways—all of which exhibit the geographical parallelism mentioned above. During the past few decades the development and population growth of the Pacific Northwest has been so enormous that the investigation of any more or less stable speech patterns may appear to be a hopeless task. Indeed, the linguistic geographer here is faced with a multitude of complex problems; but, in spite of all this, the linguistic information gradually becoming available in the files of the Linguistic Atlas of the Pacific Northwest is far from being meaningless. Here, as in California and other places already discussed, a definite correlation exists between such linguistic data and the historical processes just outlined.

On the basis of more than seven hundred mail questionnaires from all parts of Washington, Oregon, and Idaho, a fairly good sampling of vocabulary items has been made. A summary of the results follows:

(1) Words of general occurrence on the East Coast are usually common also in the Pacific Northwest. Where such items are relatively infrequent, their occurrence is complemented by a high incidence of regional variants; this is often the case in Idaho, with its preference for Northern variants, and in Oregon, which more often favors distinctly Midland variants.

Less frequent Eastern forms of general distribution are subject to even stronger competition from regional variants, again mostly of either Northern or Northern and Midland origin—with Oregon and Idaho once more proving most active in this respect. Generally infrequent in the Pacific Northwest, however, are the terms *seesaw, gutters* "eaves troughs," *burlap bag/sack* and *a bite* (to eat). Rather frequent, on the other hand, are the more or less Northern terms *skunk, co(me)/here boss(ie), shivaree, gunny bag/sack, teeter-totter,* and *baby buggy,* as well as the Midland and Southern terms *singletree, mush, second crop, bundle* (of wheat), and (*hay*) *shocks.* In addition to these more dominant terms, the non-Northern terms *coal oil, skillet, roasting ears, clabber(ed) milk, second cutting,* (*window*) *blinds, green beans,* and *hot cakes* are strong competing terms, ranging in frequency from 19 to 50 per cent.

(2) In the matter of high-frequency variants, the relative conditions prevailing in Washington, Oregon, and Idaho may be illustrated somewhat as follows:

Of the three states, Idaho has the highest frequency of Northern terms: *teeter-totter,* (*devil's*) *darning needle, outhouse, low* (of a cow), *Dutch cheese, johnny cake,* (*hay*) *cock, curtains, stoop,* and *minnies* "minnows"; Northern and Midland *drag;* and Midland (*window*) *blinds.* Idaho shows the lowest percentages in its use of the Northern and Midland terms (*hay*) *mow* and *fishworm,* the Midland terms *green beans* and *sled,* and the Midland and Southern terms *second cutting* and *bundle* (of wheat).

Washington shows relatively high occurrences of the Northern terms *quarter to, whinny, stoneboat/-bolt, sawbuck, stoop,* and *hay tumble,* and of the Midland and Southern term *second cutting,* whereas it shows the least preference for the Midland terms (*hay*) *shocks, nicker, quarter of, drag,* and *snake doctor,* and the Midland and Southern terms *skillet* and *quarter till.*

Oregon, with its decided preference for Midland terms, has the highest occurrence of the Northern term *co(me)/here boss(ie)*; the Northern and Midland term (*hay*) *mow,* and the Midland terms (*hay*) *shocks, hot cakes, sled,* (*window*) *blinds, nicker, green beans, sook(ie) boss(ie), bawl* (of a cow), *snake feeder, snake doctor;* the Midland and Southern terms *bundle* (of wheat), *clabber(ed) milk, skillet, roasting ears, quarter till, fish bait;* and the Southern (and literary) term *earthworm;* whereas there is a noticeably reduced occurrence of the Northern terms *angleworm, sick to the stomach, (devil's) darning needle, Dutch cheese, stoop, johnny cake, bellow/beller,* and the Northern and North Midland term *sawbuck,* or the Northern and Southern terms *quarter to* and *serenade.*

(3) If we consider the rarest types of variants, we find that the same general distribution holds good. Traces of Northern forms are more distinct in Washington and Idaho: for example, in Washington *whippletree, spider, minnies, whiffltree, fills/thills*—even *hasty pudding, griddle-cakes,* and *swiveltree*—are found; in Idaho, *minnies, fills/thills, whippletree, whiffletree, spider;* in Oregon, *minnies, whippletree.*

The Northern and North Midland term *whinner* occurs in Washington and Idaho, but not in Oregon, although Oregon does have the Southern (rarely New England) term *whicker.* In Midland and Southern trace-forms, Oregon again stands out with *barn lot, dog irons, thick milk, pulley bone,* and *snap beans.* Washington has a few occurrences of the first two, but otherwise both Washington and Idaho fail to share in these terms.

(4) Strictly Southern terms are always very rare in the Pacific Northwest.

(5) Typically Western terms are quite common, particularly in the southeastern parts of the area. Words like *corral,* for instance, are restricted in their distribution to the areas in which they have application.

A question of "urban unfamiliarity" in connection with many of these terms was first raised by David Reed. This is actually part of a larger problem involving literary influence. Almost all the terms in general distribution in the East, and a number of typically Northern terms, enjoy wide usage through literary media and are, therefore, open to question on grounds of urban (or rural) unfamiliarity. Dialect fusion in itself is further complicated by literary influences from specific occupational sources: The advertising manager of one large grocery chain, for example, insists on selling *roasting ears* to a public which is probably more prone to look for *corn-on-the-cob;* a certain food company markets its *pancake flour* with the term *flapjack flour* prominently displayed on the label; another sells *corn-bread* mix with directions given for making *johnny cake;* an Idaho informant claims that the source of the Idaho word for *slip* "stoneboat" is the Sears and Roebuck catalogue—as it must be for other items. The use of a descriptive term instead of some familiar dialectal variant further complicates the matter and, incidentally, makes statistical analysis difficult. While *gunny sack* is seldom referred to as *burlap bag/sack* in the Pacific Northwest, the special alternatives in the East or South (*tow sack, guano sack, sea-grass sack, croker sack,* etc.) and in California (*barley sack,* etc.) are matched by such terms as *grain sack, potato sack,* and *feed sack.*

As has already been implied on the basis of settlement history, strong regional variations are very hard to trace in the Pacific Northwest. In Washington, Midland terms occur with relatively higher frequency along the Columbia and Snake Rivers in the eastern part of the state, and they are also prominent in a few smaller areas, notably one around Bellingham. Northern terms predominate in northern Idaho, while Midland terms are more noticeable in the Snake River region; in this respect the adjacent areas of Washington and Idaho show an unbroken transition. The history of Idaho differs from that of eastern Washington only with regard to its mining areas, where a relatively large number of immigrant Irish have settled, and to its area of Mormon settlement, which seems to be slightly more homogeneous than other areas. Oregon shows clearly its Midland origins in almost all areas. The word *corral* occurs with greatest frequency in southern Idaho, then in eastern Oregon, and only sporadically in eastern Washington, so that the occurrence of this term can easily be taken as an index to the spread of a cultural phenomenon that scarcely exists west of the Cascade Mountains.

As for the coastal regions, the earliest settlements from New

England clustered around the entrances to navigable waterways —Puget Sound, Gray's Harbor, and the lower Columbia River; but since these were adjacent to timber areas, a somewhat migrant population, largely from the upper Middle West, soon spread out between them. Later on, the advent of stump-farming created an even more complex mixture in such sections, and the influx of Scandinavians and Germans changed the picture again. It is just in these regions, however, that New England relic forms seem to occur most frequently—a fact which may be a tribute to the prestige of those earliest settlers, but the possibility of Canadian influence remains to be explored.

The rather rapidly fusing character of large urban areas (from Everett to Olympia on the eastern side of Puget Sound, for example) is reflected in the fact that these areas manifest relatively few of the low-frequency variants. The most apparent evidence of dialect distribution throughout the Pacific Northwest otherwise runs according to age levels: (1) Only old people say *dog irons, serenade,* or *pie-plant;* and the terms *whinny, snake feeder, woodshed, johnny cake, smearcase, seesaw,* and *court plaster* are confined largely to old people. (2) The terms *piece* "bite to eat," *mouth organ, comb* (of the roof), *quarter of,* and *papa* are used largely by old and middle-aged speakers. (3) The terms *quarter till, polecat, cereal,* and *Band-aid*® are especially common among younger people. It is to be noted that those who prefer the terms *court plaster* and *smearcase* also suggest *adhesive tape* and *cottage cheese* as regular alternants. All along the line, therefore, the tendency seems to be towards regularization in favor of the predominant variants. The recent influx of fruit workers seems only to hasten this process, since the speech they bring with them is regarded as quaint but inimitable.

Maps 19–32 (pp. 103–116) illustrate variously the information summarized above. (See also the notes which follow them.) Below are given a series of tables demonstrating the relative frequency of Eastern vocabulary items occurring in Washington, Oregon, Idaho, and California (as far as these are known at present). Figures given for each item in each of the states listed represent percentages of total responses for the item described. Data from California are incomplete, because the questionnaire was augmented after the appearance of David Reed's article on California variants and before the survey of the Pacific Northwest was started. Especially significant differences in percentages among the Pacific Coast states are highlighted here by the italicized figures.

| | Washington | Idaho | Oregon | California |
|---|---|---|---|---|
| 1. Words of general distribution throughout the Atlantic Coast states. | | | | |
| *haystack* | 98 | 100 | 100 | 94 |
| *mantel* | 98 | 100 | 98 | |
| (*clothes*) *closet* | 97 | 97 | 96 | 98 |
| (*front*) *porch* | 97 | 96 | 87 | |
| (*just*) *a* (*little*) *way*(*s*) | 88 | 96 | 95 | 92 |
| *shafts, shavs, shays* | 98 | 95 | 100 | |
| *wishbone* | 82 | 82 | 81 | 81 |
| (*saw*) *horse* (for wood) | 77 | 85 | 86 | |
| *moo* | 61 | 58 | 62 | 59 |
| *privy* | 25 | 24 | 24 | |
| *backhouse* | 24 | *12* | 26 | |
| *faucet* | 91 | *68* | 97 | 96 |
| *corn bread* | 88 | *77* | 95 | 92 |
| *cottage cheese* | 71 | *62* | 77 | 79 |
| *dragonfly* | 66 | *49* | 66 | 61 |
| (*back*) *porch* | 61 | *41* | 60 | |
| *corn on the cob* | 67 | *66* | 49 | |
| *frying pan* | 69 | 61 | 59 | 72 |
| *seesaw* | 14 | *5* | 21 | 45 |
| *sick at the stomach* | 44 | 41 | *68* | 41 |
| *pancake* | 44 | *54* | 45 | 43 |
| 2. Words occurring in parts of the North, Midlands, and South (almost general). | | | | |
| *gutters* | 28 | 29 | 26 | *46* |
| *string beans* | 75 | 80 | *67* | 80 |
| *hay/barn loft* | 61 | 84 | *48* | 81 |
| *a bite* (to eat) | 12 | 16 | 7 | 16 |
| *snack* | 49 | *40* | 66 | 63 |
| (*window*) *shades* | 61 | 42 | 48 | *86* |
| *burlap bag/sack* | 2 | 6 | 8 | *26* |

| | | Washington | Idaho | Oregon | California |
|---|---|---|---|---|---|
| 3. | Words occurring throughout the North and Midlands. | | | | |
| | *sheaf* | 32 | 38 | 31 | |
| 4. | Words occurring in parts of the North and Midlands. | | | | |
| 4.1 | Throughout the North and North Midlands. | | | | |
| | *skunk* | 95 | 93 | 89 | 93 |
| | *quarter of* | 12 | 13 | 18 | 27 |
| | *(hay) mow* | 39 | *16* | 43 | *2* |
| | *whinny* | 68 | 52 | 46 | 43 |
| | *(hay) cock* | 0 | 17 | 3 | 18 |
| | *whinner* | 3 | 4 | 0 | |
| 4.2 | Parts of the North and Midlands. | | | | |
| | *sled* ("stoneboat") | 37 | *16* | 51 | |
| | *fish worm* | 14 | *4* | 31 | 21 |
| | *sawbuck* (for wood) | 21 | 15 | 8 | |
| | *drag* ("stoneboat") | 7 | 22 | 12 | |
| | *stone drag* ("stoneboat") | 4 | 3 | 2 | |
| 5. | Words occurring throughout the North and South. | | | | |
| | *quarter to* | 81 | 54 | *37* | 66 |
| | *baby carriage* | 13 | 13 | 13 | *23* |
| 6. | Words occurring in parts of the North and South. | | | | |
| 6.1 | Throughout the North and part of the South. | | | | |
| | *kerosene* | 57 | 60 | 58 | 64 |
| | *curtains* ("shades") | 2 | *11* | 2 | 5 |
| 6.2 | Parts of New England and the South. | | | | |
| | *low* (of a cow) | 15 | *26* | 13 | 11 |
| | *serenade* | 3 | 4 | 2 | 11 |
| | *whicker* | 2 | 0 | 0 | 0 |
| 7. | Words occurring throughout the Midlands and the South. | | | | |
| | *coal oil* | 42 | 38 | 41 | *53* |
| | *skillet* | 24 | 36 | *40* | 34 |
| | *spicket* | 2 | 2 | 1 | 2 |
| | *pulley bone* | 0 | 0 | 3 | 4 |
| | *corn pone* | 1 | 2 | 1 | 2 |
| 8. | Words occurring in parts of the Midlands and the South. | | | | |

| | | Washington | Idaho | Oregon | California |
|---|---|---|---|---|---|
| 8.1 | Everywhere south of the Mason-Dixon Line. | | | | |
| | *singletree* | 91 | 97 | 94 | |
| | *mush* | 86 | 82 | 80 | |
| | *second crop* | 51 | 58 | 53 | |
| | *bundle* (of wheat) | 50 | 37 | 62 | |
| | *clabber(ed) (milk)* | 35 | 40 | 45 | 57 |
| | *roasting ears* | 19 | 22 | *40* | |
| | *dog irons* | 4 | 0 | *7* | 2 |
| | *polecat* | 4 | 7 | 3 | |
| | *barn lot* | 1 | 0 | *9* | 2 |
| 8.2 | Virginia and West Midland. | | | | |
| | *nicker* | 16 | 23 | *37* | 26 |
| | *snake doctor* ("dragonfly") | 1 | 2 | *10* | 9 |
| | *fishing worm* | 3 | 4 | 4 | 4 |
| | *lamp oil* | 0 | 0 | 1 | 2 |
| 8.3 | Restricted parts of the Midlands and the South. | | | | |
| | *second cutting* | 48 | 38 | 45 | |
| | *quarter till* | 5 | 10 | *27* | 4 |
| | *smearcase* | 7 | 0 | 9 | 12 |
| | *a (little) piece* ("way") | 4 | 2 | 3 | 4 |
| | *fish bait* | 3 | 2 | *7* | |
| | *(hay) rick* | 2 | 0 | 1 | 2 |
| | *pile of hay* | 0 | 0 | 0 | 8 |
| 9. | Words occurring throughout the North. | | | | |
| | *come/co/here boss(ie)* | 90 | 91 | 75 | |
| | *eaves troughs* | 38 | 22 | *48* | 18 |
| | *(devil's) darning needle* | 23 | *45* | 9 | 13 |
| | *johnny cake* | 11 | *21* | 4 | 7 |
| | *spider* ("frying pan") | 5 | 3 | 1 | 4 |
| 10. | Words occurring in part of the North. | | | | |
| 10.1 | Throughout New England and in some other Northern areas. | | | | |
| | *outhouse* | 34 | *44* | 37 | |
| | *Dutch cheese* | 17 | *24* | 9 | 6 |
| | *teeter(ing) board* | 3 | 2 | 4 | *26* |
| 10.2 | Restricted parts of the North. | | | | |
| | *stoneboat/-bolt* | 51 | 44 | 35 | |
| | *hay-tumble* | 10 | 0 | 0 | 0 |

| | | Washington | Idaho | Oregon | California |
|---|---|---|---|---|---|
| | *stoop* | 10 | 10 | 6 | |
| | *bellow, beller* (of a cow) | 8 | 6 | 2 | |
| | *whippletree* | 6 | 3 | 5 | |
| | *minnies* ("minnows") | 4 | 7 | 5 | |
| 11. | Words occurring throughout the Midlands. | | | | |
| | (*window*) *blinds* | 37 | *46* | *50* | 27 |
| | *soo(k)(ie) boss(ie)* | 11 | 9 | 25 | |
| | *snake feeder* ("dragonfly") | 8 | 2 | *11* | 6 |
| | *spouts, spouting* | 2 | 4 | 1 | 1 |
| | *spigot* | 1 | 0 | 0 | 1 |
| 12. | Words occurring in part of the Midlands. | | | | |
| | *green beans* | 25 | 20 | 31 | 17 |
| | *bawl* (of a cow) | 13 | 4 | 20 | |
| | *piece* ("snack") | 12 | 14 | 10 | 6 |
| | *curdled milk* | 1 | 2 | 3 | |
| | *cruddled milk* | 0 | 0 | 2 | 3 |
| | *thick milk* | 0 | 0 | 2 | 2 |
| 13. | Words occurring throughout the South. | | | | |
| | *snap beans* | 0 | 0 | 2 | 4 |
| 14. | Words occurring in part of the South. | | | | |
| | *mosquito hawk* | 1 | 2 | 3 | 9 |
| | *earthworm* | 1 | 0 | 5 | 8 |
| | *shelf* ("mantel") | 1 | 0 | 1 | |
| | *hand irons* | 0 | 0 | 0 | 2 |
| 15. | Words of "unexpected frequency." | | | | |
| 15.1 | Primarily Northern. | | | | |
| | *angleworm* | 63 | 73 | *37* | 53 |
| | *sick to the stomach* | 49 | 53 | *29* | 46 |
| 15.2 | North and Midland. | | | | |
| | *shivaree* | 97 | 96 | 98 | *78* |
| | *gunny bag/sack* | 86 | 86 | 82 | *66* |
| | *teeter-totter* | 83 | 93 | 78 | *43* |
| | *baby buggy* | 80 | 74 | 81 | 85 |
| 15.3 | Primarily Midland. | | | | |
| | *hot cakes* | 49 | 40 | *53* | 65 |
| | (*hay*) *shocks* | 30 | 41 | *72* | 55 |

| | | Washington | Idaho | Oregon | California |
|---|---|---|---|---|---|
| 15.4 | Western. | | | | |
| | *grate* | 18 | 25 | 20 | 20 |
| | *corral* | 8 | 40 | 22 | 51 |
| | *flapjacks* | 3 | 4 | 1 | 7 |
| | *barley sack* | 0 | 0 | 0 | 6 |
| 15.5 | Ohio Valley. | | | | |
| | *rack* ("sawhorse") | 2 | 0 | 0 | |
| 15.6 | Due to urban unfamiliarity with the item. | | | | |
| | *sour(ed) milk* | 64 | 58 | 54 | 46 |
| | *breast bone* ("wishbone") | 18 | 18 | 16 | 19 |
| | *worm* ("angleworm") | 16 | 19 | 13 | 19 |
| | *drainpipes* | 15 | 26 | 15 | 26 |
| | *eaves* | 10 | 19 | 6 | 21 |
| | *hay stack* (for "shock") | 3 | 2 | 2 | 12 |
| 15.7 | Others. | | | | |
| | *tap* ("faucet") | 6 | *36* | 2 | |
| | *veranda* ("back porch") | 3 | 4 | *13* | |
| | *slip* ("stoneboat") | 0 | *3* | 0 | |

A number of maps illustrating these word distributions, as well as some involving pronunciation, were published by David Reed and myself in an article entitled "Problems of English Speech Mixture in California and Nevada" (1972). Map 33, based on that article, shows the relative frequency of two folk terms for "cottage cheese," Northern *Dutch cheese* and Midland *smearcase*. Maps 34 and 35 show areas of concentration for two terms in California and Nevada. A warm wind, or sirocco, is known throughout the Pacific Northwest, in Nevada, and in the inland regions of northern California as a *chinook*. In southern California it is called a *Santa Ana,* or *Santana.* The *chinook* wind blows inland, can become quite moist, and has a strong melting effect on the snow—if there is any. The *Santa Ana* is very dry, blowing from the interior deserts into coastal valleys. Map 35 shows the distribution of the Spanish loan-word *arroyo* "dry wash gully or canyon" in the southern region of California, coinciding generally with the location of early

Spanish missions. A very detailed elaboration of these and other examples has been published recently by Elizabeth Bright in a book entitled *A Word Geography of California and Nevada* (1971, based on her doctoral dissertation of 1967). The prevalence of Spanish terms in southern California is of special interest, of course, in relation to Atwood's observations on Texas vocabulary (see above, p. 52).

Other unique items of vocabulary characteristic of the West in general, or in local portions of the same, involve a small number of American Indian terms, such as (*salt*) *chuck* "salt water," *potlatch* "festive celebration," or *skookum* "big," all of which are still current in the Pacific Northwest, or terms handed down from early French guides and explorers, such as *coulee* "a deep, dry wash ravine," and *butte* "flat-top hill," used in the North from Minnesota to Washington and matched by *arroyo* and *mesa* in the Southwest. Occurrence of the Spanish loanword *corral* has been noted above (p. 70): its eastern limit in the North, along with other types of western vocabulary, coincides roughly with the eastern parts of the Dakotas, Nebraska, Kansas, Oklahoma, and Texas.[16]

[16] Harold Allen, *The Linguistic Atlas of the Upper Midwest,* I: 132; and E. B. Atwood, *The Regional Vocabulary of Texas,* p. 150.

CHAPTER 9

# *Black English*

One aspect of urban dialectology that has received much attention recently is that which is often referred to as "Black English." While there has been some rather energetic research in this so-called "Negro nonstandard English," the very complex and often sensitive nature of the subject has given rise to widespread, frequently questionable speculations. Partisanship has tended to replace scholarship, with the result that our knowledge of this important subject has often been obscured or misrepresented. Richard Bailey and Jay Robinson issued an appropriate caveat, in this connection, when they wrote: "Readers of presently available research into black English should be aware that most of it is fragmentary—focused on severely restricted lists of features often recorded from the speech of only a handful of informants; and much of it is biased by the pressure for quick, easy, and general application."[1]

It must be made clear to begin with that the intensity of dialect features most often included in descriptions of Black

[1] Richard Bailey and Jay Robinson, *Varieties of Present-Day English* (New York: Macmillan, 1973), p. 238.

English may vary markedly among Negro speakers, depending upon the extent of their "in-group" involvement. Many Negroes speak varieties of English that are indistinguishable from at least some varieties spoken by whites. Others are capable of assuming at will the superficial speech characteristics of the best defined in-groups, the ghettos. Current television stars, such as Bill Cosby and Flip Wilson, regularly demonstrate their skill in this subtle type of code-switching; indeed, they may even be suspected of having a supportive influence on the spread of such characteristics among receptive black audiences. Entertainer Richard Pryor, whose artful use of Black English is ever a delight to black listeners, achieves his greatest comic effect with imitations of white speech (usually that of policemen).

If we note the most general features thus involved, we are perhaps first aware of a tendency to substitute *d* or *t* sounds for the two *th* sounds of standard English, e.g., "de man," "wit iz fren'." Since this tendency is found commonly among white speakers south of "toidy toid" street in New York, as well as in the cities of Massachusetts, Connecticut, and Rhode Island, it does not provide a shibboleth for black speakers alone. Normally, however, it is accompanied, in the latter case, with vowel sounds most similar to those heard in the deep South ("ah hep 'im" for "I help him," etc.). Another common feature is the lack of an *s* ending on verb forms in the present tense, third person singular; thus, "he go," "she sing," or even "he say" and "she do" (with perfectly regular stem forms). Additionally, from the viewpoint of standard English, certain verbs may seem to lack a distinctive past tense form, e.g., "he come," "he say," or "she change." Moreover, the lack of standard English copula forms "is," "are," "was," and "were" in normal contexts is also quite striking, e.g., "he ugly," "we bad," "they over there singin' and dancin'." Of course, there are recorded instances of hypercorrection too, such as "we plays," "you takes," and "I watches," where the *s* is replaced and extended to other grammatical persons,[2] although such expressions are found extensively among white speakers too, as are indeed the abbreviated expressions "singin'" for "singing," "fren'" for "friend," etc.

Scholars have been intrigued especially by the use of *be* in expressions for habitual events, e.g., "he usually be aroun'" and "he sometimes be busy" (in contrast to nonhabitual "he busy right now"),[3] since this construction appears to support the notion that Black English has a significantly different "deep structure" than standard English. Although this and other such locutions might seem at first to be haphazard grammatical lapses, careful inspection reveals that certain basic rules, when applied to the surface forms of standard English, can produce rather widespread systematic changes in the appearance of Black English grammar. For example, certain final consonant clusters lose their last element: the change reflected in "tes'," "des'," "han'," and "buil'," for "test," "desk," "hand," and "build," also affects the tense forms "mess'," "move'," and "scratch'," for "messed," "moved," and "scratched."[4] Most people are familiar with such phenomena in the rhymes of black jazz: *man*:*hand, down*:*round, old*:*soul,* and *blind*:*time* (in which the undefined nasalization of final *n* or *m* is also illustrated). There are additional rules for the deletion of final *r* in "we're," "their,"[5] or "four"—with no trace of a compensating offglide; final *d* in "we'd," etc.; final *l* in "I'll," "he'll"; and the final consonants of "he's," or "I've." The surface form

[2] Walter A. Wolfram, *A Sociolinguistic Description of Detroit Negro Speech* (Washington, D.C.: Center for Applied Linguistics, 1969), p. 137.

[3] Ralph W. Fasold, *Tense Marking in Black English* (Arlington, Va.: Center for Applied Linguistics, 1972), pp. 150–84.

[4] Ralph Fasold and Walter Wolfram, "Some Linguistic Features of Black English," in *Language, Society, and Education. A Profile of Black English,* ed. Johanna DeStefano (Worthington, Ohio: Charles A. Jones Publishing Co., 1973), p. 118.

[5] Both "they're" and "their" are thus pronounced "they."

of a grammar employing such simple rules tends to present a set of unique features that permit us to characterize it as Black English.

Throughout the history of American literature, notable examples of Negro speech have been attested. Literary dialects of this sort are evident in the works of Mark Twain, Joel Chandler Harris, Paul Lawrence Dunbar, and William Faulkner, to name a few. The songs of Stephen Foster, as we know, were also written to reflect the characteristics of Negro speech. Among such works as these a Negro dialect is merely suggested, not consistently recorded, yet they suffice to create a convincing illusion by employing the most striking features of Black English. In recent literature, Warren Miller's superb little novel, *Cool World,*[6] illustrates the Harlem variety, though it sometimes falls short of the mark—for example, the sentence "that how he is call priest" (with "is" inserted, contrary to pattern), "fass asleep," "you be back" (for "you'll be back"), "when I push they stay push," and "Cussers Last Stan' " (with the final *t* contrary to rule also).

It has been shown in various studies (Labov, Wolfram, et al.) that such deviation from standard English is heard more extensively among poorer, less educated speakers in ghettos, i.e., in areas where an in-group feeling is strongest. Very little effort has been made to record the vocabulary of Black English, evidently because it is thought to be so ephemeral. The claim is sometimes made that as soon as white imitators begin to take over black argot the black speakers replace it with new expressions. Some of the standard white slang associated with sex, for example, either has reverse connotation in Black English or is given totally innocuous applications. The nature of a rivalry thus revealed can be seen rather obliquely in Negro terms referring to white people. In a study dating back to 1968, Edith

[6] This can be contrasted with his novel, *The Siege of Harlem,* which scarcely shows a trace of Black English in the speech of his black characters.

Folb[7] lists the following for Los Angeles: "whitey," "gray," "honky," "peckerwood," "the beast," "the devil," and "paddy." From Chicago and New York, other terms could well be added. After observing the general list of vocabulary items collected in Watts and Venice, we may note with some interest the prevalence of identical terms in Chicago's Black Belt, New York's Harlem, or even in Boston's Roxbury. Furthermore, the wide use of terms like *funky* "something unusual," *to flake* "pass out" (from drugs, etc.), and *to woof* "to talk,"[8] among white contemporaries in the cities is an indication of the needed inventiveness among black speakers in their efforts to avoid talking like "honkies." That inventiveness is, of course, a cultural asset almost unrivalled among white ethnic groups. Playing "the dozens," "rapping," or "signifying" are highly articulate games featuring the art of matched insults as developed in black ghettos.[9]

The Folb study mentions the current use of "high yelle(r)" for a rather pale-colored Negro, usually a woman; yet the term has been used in New Orleans for well over a century. A Negro catering to whites is called a "Tom" (from "Uncle Tom," and equivalent to the Chicano term "Tio Taco" in Los Angeles), and a naive, inexperienced Negro is called a "lame," as he would also be called in New York. It is possible that the influence of special groups, such as the Muslims or Black Panthers, can be cited as a force strengthening black argot. The Los Angeles study, for example, lists *bonny gonny* "What's happening?" as a Panther import from Swaheli, and probably other

[7] Edith Folb, *A Comprehensive Study of Urban Black Argot* (San Francisco: U.S. Office of Education, 1972).

[8] A term I have used for thirty years without knowing its origin other than the fact that I picked it up in Boston.

[9] See: William Labov, *Language in the Inner City,* Studies in Black English Vernacular (Philadelphia: University of Pennsylvania Press, 1972); and Thomas Kochman (ed.), *Rappin' and stylin' out* (Urbana: University of Illinois Press, 1972).

terms of this type have their vogue, though they are admittedly difficult to illicit in planned interviews.

Much of the scholarly controversy now current regarding the nature of Black English has focused upon its possible origin. A whole group of writers (Dillard, Stewart, B. Bailey, et al.) contend that African slaves first learned a pidgin English, then developed an English creole patois preserving the African substratum, and that they maintained this as the basic language during subsequent periods of uneven, but gradual "decreolization." Others have taken sharp exception to such claims, requiting the offhand slights of the first group with studied sarcasm. They would rather derive Black English solely from implanted colonial English of the deep South. More sober minds find virtue and also logic in both points of view. This controversy should serve to warn us, however, that prejudice can hardly be substituted for evidence.

The similarity of Black English features among inhabitants of widely separated urban ghettos may owe something to modern communication between black groups. A striking uniformity in basic characteristics, however, has evidently resulted from mass labor migration from specific areas of the South, beginning after World War I, but having its greatest impact following World War II. Thus, older Negro populations in the North were augmented and eventually overwhelmed in the process. The growth of integrated public housing also helped establish new centers to accommodate the more recent migrations. Detroit, Chicago, and Los Angeles consequently developed a familiar type of in-group culture. Washington, D.C., though similarly subject to a growing black population, appears to have remained more conservative. In Boston, the evidence of Black English widely heralds the new arrivals, known as "homeys" among the older residents of Roxbury. Studies in Texas and Seattle seem to indicate certain differences in the prevalence of characteristic "black" features, however, and two possible reasons may suggest themselves, namely, the varying proportions of new and old black inhabitants, and the slightly different origins of the newcomers in various centers.

Those who place great emphasis on the creole nature of early Black English argue that segregation developed an in-group consciousness and that, as long as Negroes were movable chattel, regional or local dialects failed to gain significance. Arguments have been raised also regarding the development of language among original field slaves and house slaves. Negroes in the household of Thomas Jefferson, for example, appear to have learned to read and write; they stayed with the household over the years, while field hands were the first to be sold when financial woes were pressing.

In the various literary specimens of Negro speech available to us, nevertheless, we note many similarities with the features of Black English as heard today in the ghettos. Still there are some strikingly systematic deviations evident in individual pieces of literature. "Decreolization" in particular ways becomes a less meaningful explanation when we consider the varying regional provenience of characters quoted in the writings of Paul Lawrence Dunbar, Stephen Foster, and Mark Twain, as compared to those of William Faulkner and Joel Chandler Harris.

While the conservatism of southern Negro speech is abundantly clear to us from the records of the Linguistic Atlas, a translation of this conservatism to the modern ghetto is less acceptable to scholars who wish to see here a dynamic resurgence of some latent African substratum. The regional aspects of Black English are nonetheless undeniable, though they are obscured by the complex levels of modern urban society. Differences in the nature of Black English then, as suggested above, are dependent upon varieties of in-group participation, educational success, economic stratification, or even the sociology of the sexes—factors which influence the texture of urban speech in general beyond the equally important considerations of ethnic tradition.

CHAPTER 10

# Urban Dialects

Studies of English spoken in larger cities are normally assigned to the domain of sociolinguistics, the aim of which is to discover those dialect features that serve most significantly as indices in the delineation of social groups. From this point of view, regional distributions of language are treated as incidental; economic, occupational, ethnic, or religious entities are regarded as more relevant. Black English, for example, represents a combination of linguistic features characterizing a racial group, within which levels of economic privilege also affect the density of dialect representation. Other ethnic groups in the big cities cultivate similar in-group characteristics, exhibiting simultaneously their economic stratification or geographic cohesion.

Generally speaking, however, most urban areas reflect the basic dialect features of the surrounding countryside. As has been previously mentioned, migrations from the cities, when not strictly confined to nearby suburbia, tend to be directed towards other cities. A segment of Boston population, predominantly of Irish descent, still forms part of the older settlement in San Francisco. New Yorkers have, in the past, contributed heavily to the settlement of Chicago as well as to significant areas of Los Angeles and San Francisco. (The

Jewish district of west Los Angeles, for instance, is especially notable for its perpetuation of New York City speech.) An early New England settlement of the Puget Sound area has left little trace in the speech of Seattle, but the smaller, more isolated village of Port Townsend still maintains its original linguistic identity. Descriptions of urban speech, nevertheless—including evidence from the Linguistic Atlas—largely confirm the impression that city dialects are simply more concentrated extensions of the rural speech around them. This is especially noticeable in the cities of the West. Puget Sound, for example, has been described as "one continuous city" from Olympia to the Canadian border, and this description is appropriate particularly for the dialect, while the population density is far below that in the equivalent space between New York and Boston, where dialect differences are quite strongly marked.

Urban speech differs from its rural counterparts to the extent that its daily application is more intense, more subject to peer-group confirmation through usage and, at the same time, readily accessible to innovation, particularly in response to the pressures of commerce. In a geographical scheme of dialect distribution, therefore, cities tend to exhibit at least some small features of unique identity. The city of Boston and its environs have been identified, for instance, with their use of the word *tonic* "soda water" (any flavor). In a somewhat greater radius, the shibboleth *pahk the cah-r-in the pahk* features a unique *ah* sound approaching that of the *a* in *cat*.

New York is likewise the geographic hub for certain items of vocabulary—*pot cheese* "cottage cheese," for example. It also preserves the "dropped-*r*" in contrast to those "*r*-ful" dialects of surrounding regions. Moreover, some speakers in New York also have a peculiar *uh-ee* diphthong in words like thirty (heard by others as *thoidy*—or *toidy*), which is also used in South Carolina as well as in the vicinity of New Orleans.

In and around Philadelphia, *pavement* "sidewalk," *baby coach* "baby carriage," *paled fence* "picket fence," and *bagged school* "skipped school" are fairly localized. Professor Harold

Allen has noted a few localisms too around Minneapolis and St. Paul; for example, *rubber binder* "rubber band"—a very old expression which seems to be enjoying revival now among younger speakers. Puget Sound's "continuous city," with Seattle in the middle, is characterized only by its use of Salishan Indian terms (mentioned above) and its not always orthodox pronunciations of place names, such as *pew-allop* for Puyallop.

In California both the San Francisco and Los Angeles areas (like Las Vegas, Nevada) have a simple *e* sound in *egg* which contrasts to the *ay-ee* pronunciation (like *ague*) in the surrounding countryside. The same is true regarding the pronunciation of *on,* with (northern) *ahn* in the cities contrasted to *awn* in the ranchlands. The extent to which commercialism is infectious can also be seen in the use of *butterhorn* "Danish pastry" in San Francisco and Los Angeles (it is also the regular form in Seattle), and *snail* throughout northern California (as well as in Portland, Oregon). Northern California also uses the term *chesterfield* for "sofa," which appears to have begun with a single urban vendor of parlor refinements some time in the not too remote past.

The effect of urban speech on a surrounding region, as well as the influence of cultivated speech upon that of less "advantaged" speakers, was aptly illustrated by Professor Raven I. McDavid, Jr., in his article "The Position of the Charleston Dialect."[1] Since that time a number of attempts have been made to study the relation of dialect indicators to the sociology of larger urban centers. In his book *The Pronunciation of English in Metropolitan Chicago,* Lee A. Pederson, a professor of English at Emory University, undertook such an investigation, using the conventional means of the Linguistic Atlas supplemented by specific inquiries aimed at discovering correlations between social differences and certain recurrent features of pronunciation. In the resulting data he was able to discern a

[1] In *Publication of the American Dialect Society,* No. 23 (1955), 35–49, reprint in Williamson and Burke, 596–609.

group of distinctive features common to the speech of native Negroes in Metropolitan Chicago as opposed to the dispersion of such features among Caucasians in the same city. Among those noted were the pronunciations of *wheat, whip* and *wheelbarrow* with an initial *hw-* rather than simply *w-,* the sounding of *s* in *grease* and *greasy* with a *z,* and the sound of *yeast* like that of the word *east.* Whereas these and other features were rather uniformly represented in Negro speech, they were found distributed among white speakers according to such criteria as geography, education, age, economic privilege, and religious contact. Pederson's methods and results not only achieved initial, pioneering success in the study of urban speech, but they pointed the way for further kinds of investigation in this direction.

A much more ambitious project was carried out at the same time by Professor William Labov, now at the University of Pennsylvania, dealing with the city of New York. His book *The Social Stratification of English in New York City* (1966) describes the extremely meticulous methods by which he was able to exercise control of the vast amount of linguistic material here assembled. In this work again we find significant correlations between dialect features and those of geography, education, economic status, ethnic awareness, and age grouping. The most interesting part of this study, apart from its versatility in the collection of details, is its contribution to the concept of linguistic change as a feature of group psychology. Not only do we see here the familiar characteristics of "upward mobility" —so common to immigrant populations—or the in-group conformity of ethnic neighborhoods, but also the preservation of various dialect levels in conformance with attested scales of economic values. Thus, the department store personnel, upstairs and downstairs, in uptown and downtown stores, as well as their customers, display certain distinctions that correspond to price and service, and also, of course, to the areas served. Incidence of the post-vocalic *r* in the words *fourth floor,* for example, is more prominent among floorwalkers than among stockboys. "Lower classes" are identified with pronunciations like *goil, woild* for "girl," "world," or like *toidy toid* for "thirty third," and with the more exaggerated diphthongs in *cay-uh* "care" and *boh-uhd* "board." While upward mobility encourages Negro speakers from the ghetto to adapt their speech accordingly, and so-called "southern speech" has long been identified with white oppression, there is also a negative force inducing conformity to the usage of an ethnic majority with all its notably "southern" characteristics. Thus, the sociological nature of a complex urban environment tends to preserve dialect levels or areas while yielding at the same time, to the pressures of economic advantage. The consequence appears to be that members of a large urban society share the features of various sub-groups and are able to shift linguistically, more or less at will, from the characteristics of one group to those of another, depending upon their experience and motivation.

Obviously, a great deal more research is needed in matters of this kind and in the manner initiated by Pederson and Labov. It has been observed that language itself can severely limit the economic opportunities of its speakers, not only individuals, but entire groups. A detailed knowledge of dialect features used in the cities, therefore, could well reveal at least one type of therapy for the treatment of urban ills.

CHAPTER 11

# Future of American Dialect Studies

The description of dialect conditions in the United States, especially in the Western states, has been brief and sketchy. While vocabulary studies have been greatly facilitated by correspondence questionnaires, information is still conspicuously lacking for a good many parts of the country.

Published works of Hans Kurath, the late Bernard Bloch, the late E. B. Atwood, Harold Allen, and Raven I. McDavid, Jr., on the speech of the Eastern coastal states now constitute our principal source of information on American dialects. As we have seen, the data contained therein is all-important for the study of areas further west. Even in itself, however, this material provides us with an excellent background for linguistic research. Audrey Duckert, of the University of Massachusetts, for example, has begun to make new recordings of New England speakers in order to study the changes that have taken place there in the last thirty years,[1] and William Labov, of Columbia University, has made

[1] Audrey Duckert, "The Linguistic Atlas of New England Revisited," *Publication of the American Dialect Society,* No. 39 (April, 1963), pp. 8–15.

use of recordings from Martha's Vineyard (Mass.) as a means of calculating the effect of socio-linguistic factors on language change.[2] Undoubtedly many more such interesting research efforts will be generated, particularly after information becomes available from other Atlas sources. Materials from the entire Middle West are, of course, available in archives. Most of the states along the Mississippi have also been studied to some extent. The Rocky Mountain areas in and around Colorado, all of California, Nevada, Washington, and Idaho have been investigated through personal field work.

A great deal of editing is necessary before the results of such research can be made available for study. The chief deterrents—as in so many cases of scholarly endeavor—are the lack of qualified persons to do the job and a shortage of research funds. Most of the work now in progress owes its existence to the individual sacrifices of devoted scholars. If they persist in their efforts, however, perhaps the Linguistic Atlas of the United States will someday be complete.

Originally this project was intended to include Canada, but no organized effort in that direction got under way until a few years ago. Now there is a real possibility that a comprehensive study of the English language in North America will be made.

Chief contributors to the study of Canadian English have been Professors Walter S. Avis and H. R. Wilson, both of the Royal Military College (Ontario), although a number of other Canadian scholars are now actively engaged in research on the subject.[3]

The recognition of individuality in speech and its provenience has already begun to serve many fields of science, from sociometry and psychotherapy to semantics and literary criticism. In the course of our dialect survey we have seen how closely all the factors of our historical background and culture contribute to make language what it is in time and space. By examining the

[2] William Labov, "The Social Motivation of a Sound Change," *Word,* XIV (Dec., 1963), 273–309.

[3] See the Bibliography.

precedents of history, we learn to predict the future. If we observe dispassionately the course of language history, we shall soon cease to fear change and adaptation and learn to make use of both. More than this, we shall come to appreciate and cherish the values of creative expression and of linguistic individualism and to protect them from the violence of mass regimentation.

# *A Selected Bibliography*


Alexander, Henry. *The Story of Our Language,* rev. ed. New York: Doubleday & Company, Inc., 1962.

Allen, Harold B. "Minor Dialect Areas of the Upper Midwest," *Publication of the American Dialect Society,* No. 30 (Nov., 1958), pp. 3–16.

———. "Canadian-American Speech Differences Along the Middle Border," *Journal of the Canadian Linguistic Association,* V, i (Spring, 1959), 17–24.

Atwood, E. B. "A Preliminary Report on Texas Word Geography," *Orbis,* II (Jan., 1953), 61–66.

———. *A Survey of Verb Forms in the Eastern United States.* Ann Arbor: University of Michigan Press, 1953.

———. "The Methods of American Dialectology," *Zeitschrift für Mundartforschung,* XXX (Oct., 1963), 1–30.

———. *The Regional Vocabulary of Texas.* Austin: University of Texas Press, 1962.

Avis, Walter S. "The Mid-Back Vowels in the English of the Eastern United States: A Detailed Investigation of Regional and Social Differences in Phonic Characteristics and

Phonemic Organization." Doctoral dissertation, University of Michigan, 1956; microfilm.

———. "Speech Differences Above the Ontario–United States Border," *Journal of the Canadian Linguistic Association,* I, i (Oct., 1954), 13–17; I, i (Regular Series, March, 1956), 14–19; II, ii (Oct., 1956), 41–59.

Babington, Mima, and E. B. Atwood. "Lexical Usage in Southern Louisiana," *Publication of the American Dialect Society,* No. 36 (Nov., 1961), pp. 1–24.

Barrows, S. T. "Watch, Water, Wash," *American Speech,* IV (April, 1929), 301–302.

Baugh, Albert C. *A History of the English Language.* New York: Appleton-Century-Crofts, 1957.

Bloomfield, Leonard. *Language.* New York: Holt, Rinehart and Winston, Inc., 1933.

Brengelman, F. H. "The Native American English Spoken in the Puget Sound Area." Doctoral dissertation, University of Washington, 1957.

Brooks, Cleanth, Jr. *The Relation of the Alabama-Georgia Dialect to the Provincial Dialects of Great Britain.* Baton Rouge: Louisiana State University Press, 1935.

Cassidy, F. G. "Some New England Words in Wisconsin," *Language,* XVII (Oct.–Dec., 1941), 324–339.

Clough, W. O. "Some Wyoming Speech Patterns," *American Speech,* XXIX (Feb., 1954), 28–35.

Davis, A. L. "A Word Atlas of the Great Lakes Region." Doctoral dissertation, University of Michigan, 1948; microfilm.

Davis, A. L., and R. I. McDavid, Jr. "*Shivaree:* An Example of Cultural Diffusion," *American Speech,* XXIV (1949), 249–255.

DeCamp, David. "The Pronunciation of English in San Francisco," *Orbis,* VII (June, 1958), 372–391; VIII (Jan., 1959), 54–77.

Duckert, Audrey R. "The Linguistic Atlas of New England Revisited," *Publication of the American Dialect Society,* No. 39 (April, 1963), pp. 8–15.

Dunbar, Gary S. "A Southern Geographical Word List," *American Speech,* XXXVI (Dec., 1961), 293–296.

Francis, W. N. *The Structure of American English.* (With a chapter on American English Dialects by Raven I. McDavid, Jr.) New York: The Ronald Press Company, 1958.

Hall, Robert A., Jr. *Linguistics and Your Language,* rev. ed. New York: Doubleday & Company, Inc., 1960.

Hankey, Clyde T. "Semantic Features and Eastern Relics in Colorado Dialect," *American Speech,* XXXVI (Dec., 1961), 266–270.

———. "A Colorado Word Geography," *Publication of the American Dialect Society,* No. 34 (Nov., 1960).

Hubbell, Allan F. *The Pronunciation of English in New York City.* New York: Kings Crown Press, 1950.

Jackson, Elizabeth H. "An Analysis of Certain Colorado Atlas Field Records with Regard to Settlement History and Other Factors." Doctoral dissertation, University of Colorado, 1956; microfilm.

Jesperson, Otto. *Growth and Structure of the English Language,* 9th ed. Oxford: Blackwell, 1952.

Kerr, Elizabeth M., and Ralph M. Aderman. *Aspects of American English.* New York: Harcourt, Brace & World, Inc., 1963. Useful bibliography.

Kimmerle, M. M., R. I. McDavid, Jr., and V. G. McDavid. "Problems of Linguistic Geography in the Rocky Mountain Area," *Western Humanities Review,* V (Summer, 1951), 249–264.

Kurath, Hans. *Handbook of the Linguistic Geography of New England.* Providence: Brown University Press, 1939.

———. "Dialect Areas, Settlement Areas and Cultural Areas in the United States," in *The Cultural Approach to History,* ed. C. F. Ware. New York: Columbia University Press, 1940, pp. 331–351.

———. *A Word Geography of the Eastern United States.* Ann Arbor: University of Michigan Press, 1949.

Kurath, Hans, and R. I. McDavid, Jr. *The Pronunciation of English in the Atlantic States.* Ann Arbor: University of Michigan Press, 1961.

Labov, William. "The Social Motivation of a Sound Change," *Word* XIX (Dec., 1963), 273–309.

McDavid, R. I., Jr. "Linguistic Geography in Canada: An Introduction," *Journal of the Canadian Linguistic Association,* I, i (Oct., 1954), 3–8.

———, ed. *The American Language* by H. L. Mencken, abridged ed. New York: Alfred A. Knopf, Inc., 1963. See especially the section on dialects, pp. 448–478.

McDavid, R. I., Jr., and V. G. McDavid. "Grammatical Differences in the North Central States," *American Speech,* XXXV (Feb., 1960), 5–19.

McDavid, R. I., Jr., and V. G. McDavid. "Regional Linguistic Atlases in the United States," *Orbis,* V (June, 1956), 349–386.

McDavid, V. G. "Verb Forms in the North-Central States and the Upper Midwest." Doctoral dissertation, University of Minnesota, 1956; microfilm.

*The March of Civilization in Maps and Pictures.* New York: C. S. Hammond & Co., Inc., 1957.

Marckwardt, A. H. "Middle English *o* in American English of the Great Lakes Area," *Papers of the Michigan Academy of Science,* XXVI (1941), 561–571.

———. "Middle English *wa* in the Speech of the Great Lakes Region," *American Speech,* XVII (Dec., 1942), 226–234.

———. "Principal and Subsidiary Dialect Areas in the North-Central States," *Publication of the American Dialect Society,* No. 27 (April, 1957), pp. 3–15.

———. *American English.* New York: Oxford University Press, Inc., 1958.

Mencken, H. L. *The American Language,* 4th ed. New York: Alfred A. Knopf, Inc., 1936. Supplement I, 1946. Supplement II, 1948.

Miller, William. *A History of the United States.* New York: Dell Publishing Co., Inc., 1958.

Mills, R. V. "Oregon Speechways," *American Speech,* XXV (May, 1950), 81–90.

Nevins, Allan, and H. S. Commager. *A Pocket History of the United States.* New York: Pocket Books, Inc., 1956.

O'Hare, Thomas J. "The Linguistic Geography of Eastern Montana." Doctoral dissertation, University of Texas, 1964; microfilm.

Orton, Harold, and Eugen Dieth. *Survey of English Dialects.* Leeds: E. J. Arnold and Son, Ltd., 1962–

Paullin, C. O., and J. K. Wright. *Atlas of the Historical Geography of the United States.* New York and Washington: American Geographical Society and Carnegie Institute, 1952.

Pearce, T. M. "Three Rocky Mountain Terms: park, sugan and plaza," *American Speech,* XXXIII (May, 1958), 99–107.

Potter, Simeon, *Our Language.* Harmondsworth, Middlesex: Penguin Books, Ltd., 1950.

Pyles, Thomas. *Words and Ways of American English.* New York: Random House, Inc., 1952.

Reed, C. E. "What Is Linguistics?" *German Quarterly,* XXV (Jan., 1952), 16–25.

———. "The Pronunciation of English in the State of Washington," *American Speech,* XXVII (Oct., 1952), 186–189.

———. "Washington Words," *Publication of the American Dialect Society,* No. 25 (April, 1956), pp. 3–11.

———. "Word Geography of the Pacific Northwest," *Orbis,* VI (Jan.–June, 1957), 82–89.

———. "Frontiers of English in the Pacific Northwest," *Proceedings of the 9th Pacific Northwest Conference of Foreign Language Teachers* (April, 1958), pp. 33–35.

———. "The Pronunciation of English in the Pacific Northwest," *Language,* XXVII (Oct.–Dec., 1961), 559–564.

Reed, D. W. "Eastern Dialect Words in California," *Publication of the American Dialect Society,* No. 21 (April, 1954), pp. 3–15.

Robertson, Stuart, and Frederic G. Cassidy. *The Development of Modern English.* Englewood Cliffs, N.J.: Prentice-Hall, Inc., 1954.

Scargill, M. H. "Sources of Canadian English," *Journal of English and Germanic Philology,* LVI (Oct., 1957), 610–614.

Thomas, C. K. "The Dialectal Significance of the Non-Phonemic Low-Back Vowel Variants Before *R,*" in *Studies in Speech and Drama in Honor of Alexander M. Drummond.* Ithaca, N.Y., 1944.

———. "Notes on the Pronunciation of 'Hurry,' " *American Speech,* XXI (April, 1946), 114.

———. *An Introduction to the Phonetics of American English,* 2nd ed. New York: The Ronald Press Company, 1958.

Trager, G. L. *The Field of Linguistics* (*Studies in Linguistics,* Occasional Papers, No. 1). Norman, Okla.: Battenburg Press, 1949.

Turner, F. J. *The Frontier in American History.* Henry Holt and Co., Inc., 1920.

Turner, L. D. "Notes on the Sounds and Vocabulary of Gullah," *Publication of the American Dialect Society,* No. 3 (May, 1945), pp. 13–28.

———. "Problems Confronting the Investigator of Gullah," *Publication of the American Dialect Society,* No. 9 (April, 1948), pp. 74–84.

Wertenbaker, Thomas J. *The American People: A History.* New York: Charles Scribner's Sons, 1926.

Wetmore, Thomas H. "The Low-Central and Low-Back Vowels in the English of the Eastern United States," *Publication of the American Dialect Society,* No. 32 (Nov., 1959).

Wilson, H. R. "The Dialect of Lunenburg County, Nova Scotia." Doctoral dissertation, University of Michigan, 1958; microfilm.

Wood, Gordon R. "An Atlas Survey of the Interior South (U.S.A.)," *Orbis,* IX (Jan., 1960), 7–12.

———. "Word Distribution in the Interior South," *Publication of the American Dialect Society,* No. 35 (April, 1961), 1–16.

Wyld, H. C. *A Short History of English,* 2nd ed. London: John Murray, 1921.

*Addenda*

Allen, Harold B. *The Linguistic Atlas of the Upper Midwest.* [LAUM] 2 vols. Minneapolis: University of Minnesota Press, 1973–75.

Allen, Harold B. and Gary N. Underwood, eds. *Readings in American Dialectology.* New York: Appleton-Century, Crofts, 1971.

Bailey, Beryl L. "Toward a New Perspective in Negro English Dialectology." In Wolfram and Clarke, 41–50; and in Allen and Underwood, 421–27.

Bailey, Richard and Jay L. Robinson. *Varieties of Present-Day English.* New York: Macmillan, 1973.

Bright, Elizabeth S. *A Word Geography of California and Nevada.* Berkeley and Los Angeles: University of California Press, 1971.

Carlson, David R. *The Common Speech of Boston.* Dissertation: University of Massachusetts, Amherst, 1973.

Davis, Lawrence M. "Dialect Research: Mythology vs. Reality," *Orbis,* XVIII (1969), 332–37. In Wolfram and Clarke, 90–98.

———, ed. *Studies in Linguistics in Honor of Raven I. McDavid, Jr.* University, Ala.: University of Alabama Press, 1972.

DeStefano, Johanna, ed. *Language, Society, and Education. A Profile of Black English.* Worthington, Ohio: Charles A. Jones Publishing Co., 1973.

Dillard, J. L. *Black English. Its History and Usage in the United States.* New York: Random House, 1972.

Fasold, Ralph W. *Tense Marking in Black English.* Arlington, Va.: Center for Applied Linguistics, 1972.

Fasold, Ralph W. and Walter Wolfram. "Some Linguistic Features of Black English." In DeStefano, 116–48.

Folb, Edith. *A Comprehensive Study of Urban Black Argot.* San Francisco: U.S. Office of Education, March, 1972.

Houston, Susan. "A Sociolinguistic Consideration of the Black English of Children in Northern Florida," *Language,* XLV (1969), 599–607.

Kochman, Thomas, ed. *Rappin' and Stylin' Out.* Urbana: University of Illinois Press, 1972.

Labov, William. *Language in the Inner City.* Studies in Black English Vernacular. Philadelphia: University of Pennsylvania Press, 1972.

———. *The Social Stratification of English in New York City.* Washington, D.C.: Center for Applied Linguistics, 1966.

———. "Some Features of the English of Black Americans." In Bailey and Robinson, 236–55.

Labov, William and Paul Cohen. "Systematic Relations of Standard and Non-Standard Rules in the Grammar of Negro Speakers." In DeStefano, 149–60.

Loflin, Marvin D. "Negro Nonstandard and Standard English:

Same or Different Deep Structure?", *Orbis,* XVIII (1969), 74–91.

———. "On the Structure of the Verb in a Dialect of American Negro English." In Allen and Underwood, 428–43.

McDavid, Raven I., Jr. "The Position of the Charleston Dialect," *Publication of the American Dialect Society,* No. 23 (1955), 35–49. In Williamson and Burke, 596–609.

McDavid, Raven I., Jr., and Virginia G. McDavid. "The Relationship of the Speech of American Negroes to the Speech of Whites." In Wolfram and Clarke, 16–40.

Parslow, Robert L. "The Pronunciation of English in Boston, Massachusetts: Vowels and Consonants." In Williamson and Burke, 610–24.

Pederson, Lee A. "Non-Standard Negro Speech in Chicago." In Stewart 1964, 16–20.

———. "The Pronunciation of English in Metropolitan Chicago." University, Ala.: *Publication of the American Dialect Society,* No. 23, University of Alabama Press, 1955. In Williamson and Burke, 525–48.

———. "Some Structural Differences in the Speech of Chicago Negroes." In Allen and Underwood, 401–20.

Reed, Carroll E. and David W. Reed. "Problems of English Speech Mixture in California and Nevada," *Studies in Linquistics in Honor of Raven I. McDavid, Jr.* University, Ala.: University of Alabama Press, 1972, 135–43.

Stewart, William A. "Continuity and Change in American Negro Dialects." In Allen and Underwood, 454–67; and in Wolfram and Clarke, 51–73.

———. "Sociolinguistic Factors in the History of American Negro Dialects." In Wolfram and Clarke, 74–89.

———. "Urban Negro Speech: Sociolinguistic Factors Affecting English Teaching." In DeStefano, 161–65.

———, ed. *Non-standard Speech and the Teaching of English.* Washington, D.C.: Center for Applied Linguistics, 1964.

Williamson, Juanita V. "A Phonological and Morphological

Study of the Speech of the Negro of Memphis, Tennessee," *Publication of the American Dialect Society,* No. 50, University of Alabama Press, 1968.

Williamson, Juanita and Virginia M. Burke, eds. *A Various Language. Perspectives on American Dialects.* New York: Holt, Rinehart, and Winston, 1971.

Wolfram, Walter. "Black-White Speech Differences Revisited." In Wolfram and Clarke, 139–61.

———. *A Sociological Description of Detroit Negro Speech.* Washington, D.C.: Center for Applied Linguistics, 1969.

Wolfram, Walter and Nona H. Clarke, eds. *Black-White Speech Relationships.* Washington, D.C.: Center for Applied Linguistics, 1971.

# *Maps and Notes to Maps*

## *Acknowledgments*

From Hans Kurath, *A Word Geography of the Eastern United States* (Ann Arbor: University of Michigan Press, Copyright © 1949), Figures 3, 125, 23, 141, 41–42, 30, 25. Figures 3 and 23 are virtually unchanged in form; new maps have been made combining isoglosses taken from others cited.

From E.B. Atwood, *A Survey of Verb Forms in the Eastern United States* (Ann Arbor: University of Michigan Press, Copyright © 1953). Figures 17 and 26 are used to project isoglosses on two maps identical with the Atwood base map.

From W. Nelson Francis, *The Structure of American English* (New York: The Ronald Press, Copyright © 1958), map 6 on page 585 which was prepared by Mrs. Raven I. McDavid, Jr.

From Marjorie M. Kimmerle, Raven I. McDavid, Jr., and Virginia G. McDavid, *Problems of Linguistic Geography in the Rocky Mountain Area (The Western Humanities Review,* Volume V, Number 3, Summer, 1951) adapted and reprinted from page 254 with permission of the editor and the authors.

From David W. Reed and Carroll E. Reed, "Problems of Speech Mixture in California and Nevada," *Studies in Honor of Raven I. McDavid, Jr.* (University, Alabama: University of Alabama Press, 1972), maps 33, 34, and 35, on pages 130–32.

## MAP NO. 1

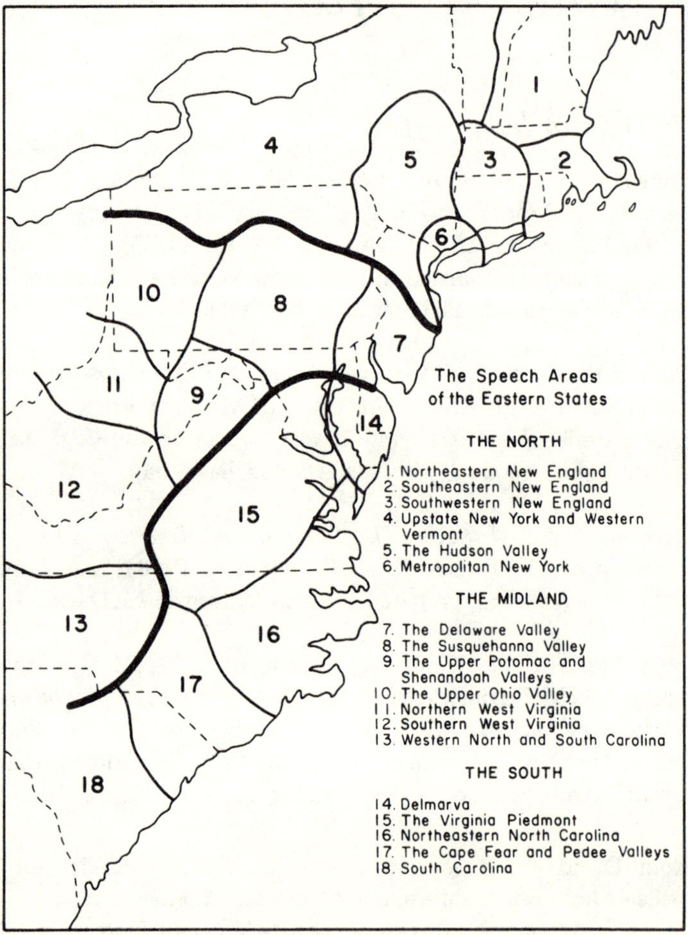


Reprinted from *A Word Geography of the Eastern United States* by Hans Kurath.

# MAP NO. 2

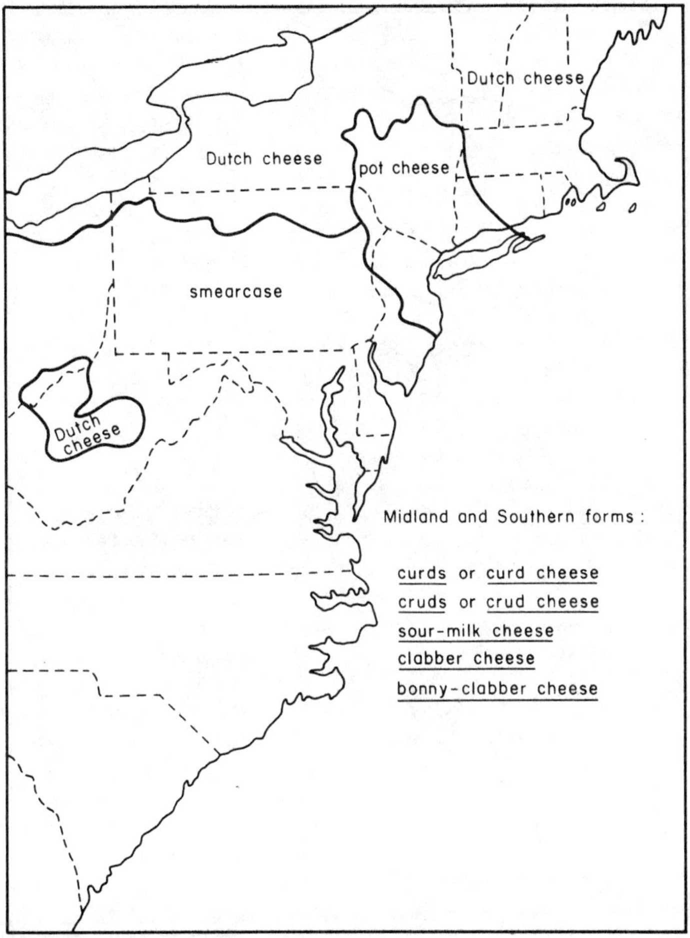


Reprinted from *A Word Geography of the Eastern United States* by Hans Kurath.

## MAP NO. 3

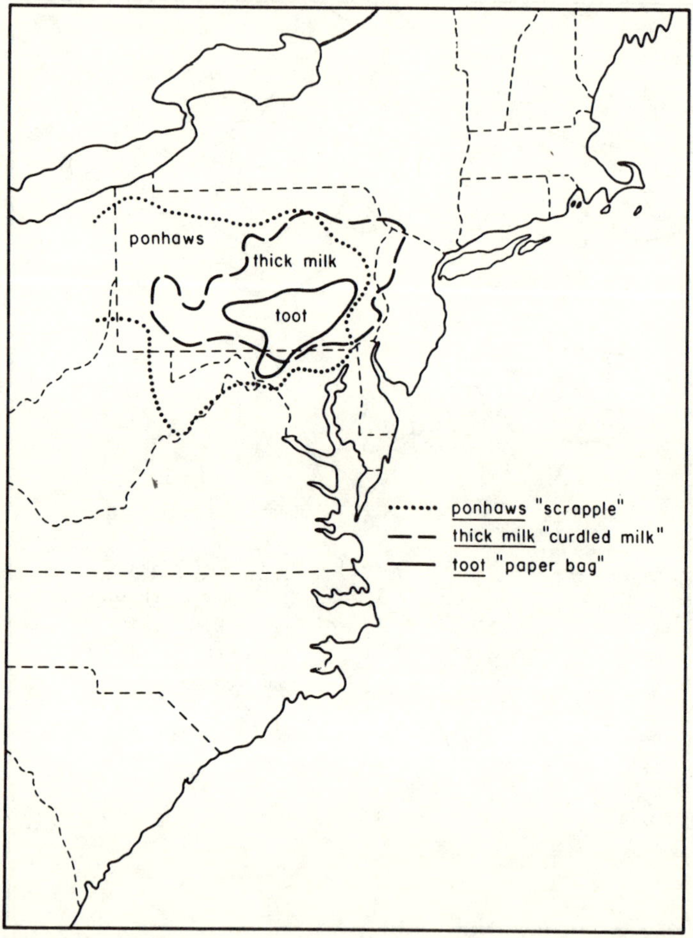


Reprinted from *A Word Geography of the Eastern United States* by Hans Kurath.

## MAP NO. 4

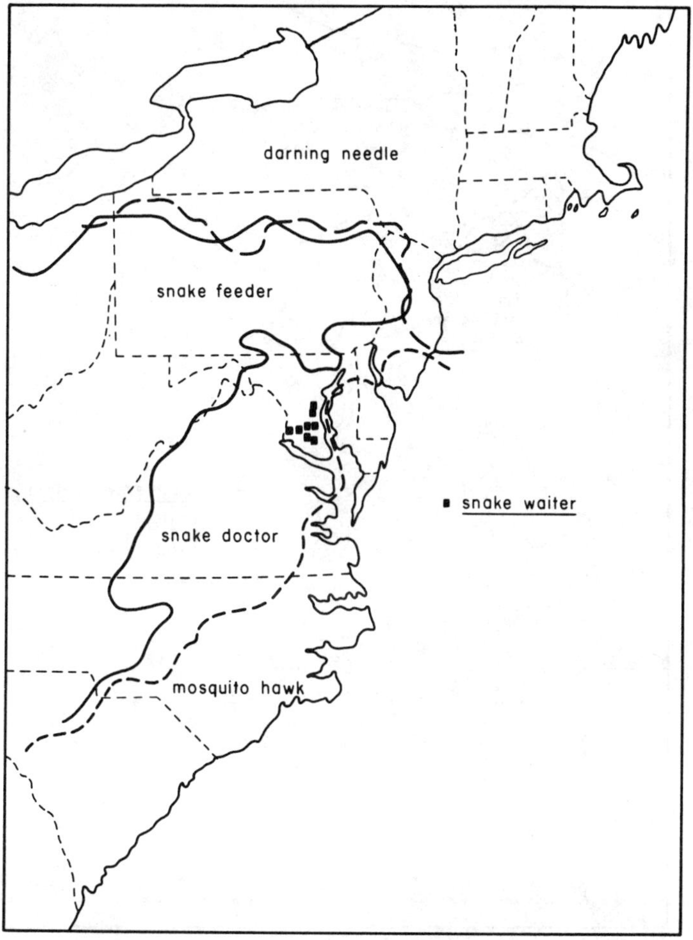


Reprinted from *A Word Geography of the Eastern United States* by Hans Kurath.

# MAP NO. 5

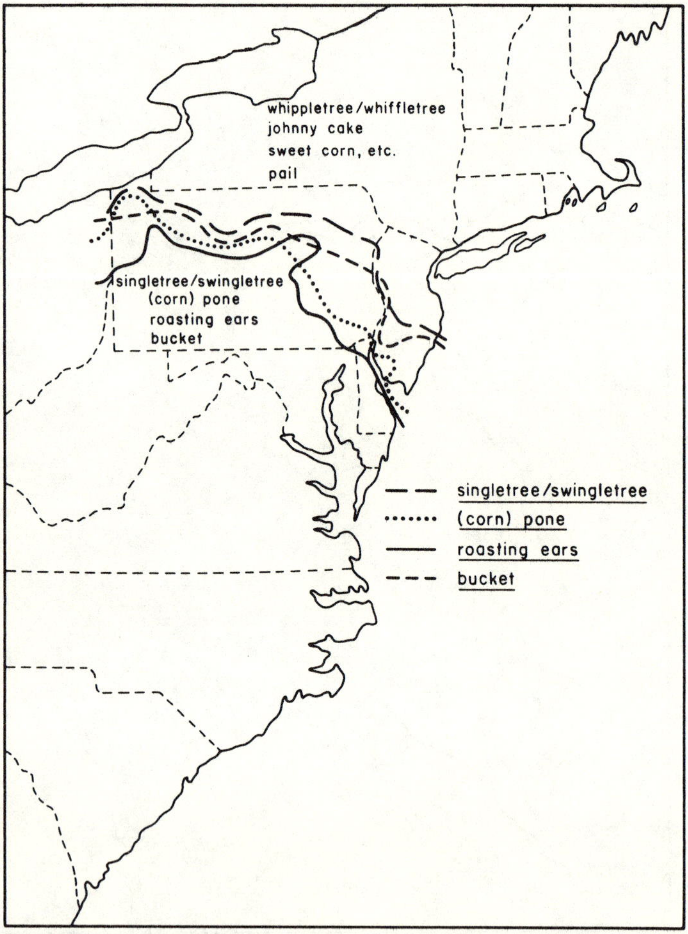


Reprinted from *A Word Geography of the Eastern United States* by Hans Kurath.

# MAP NO. 6

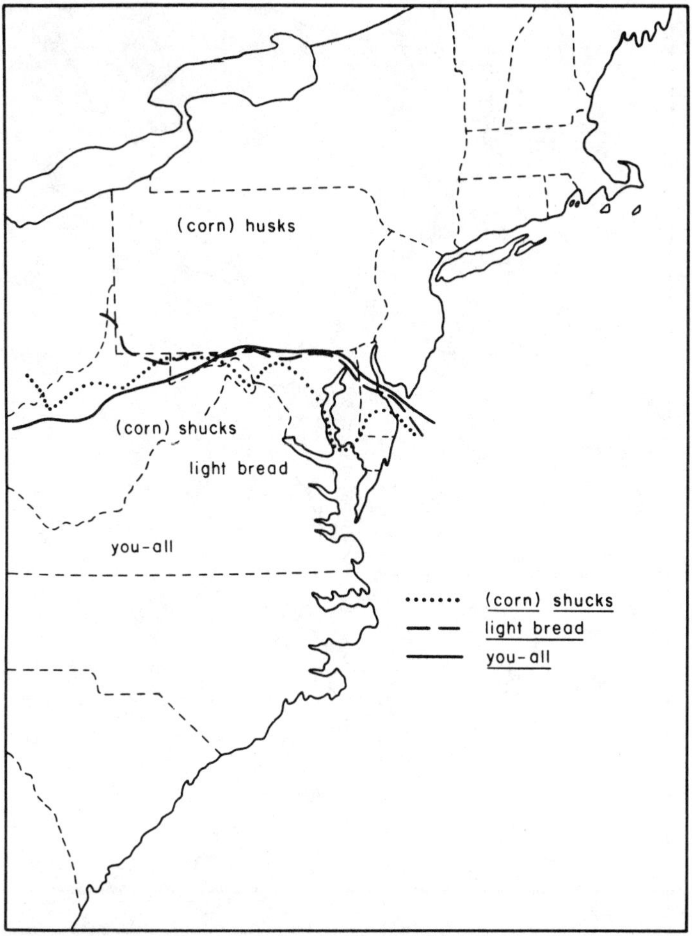


Reprinted from *A Word Geography of the Eastern United States* by Hans Kurath.

## MAP NO. 7

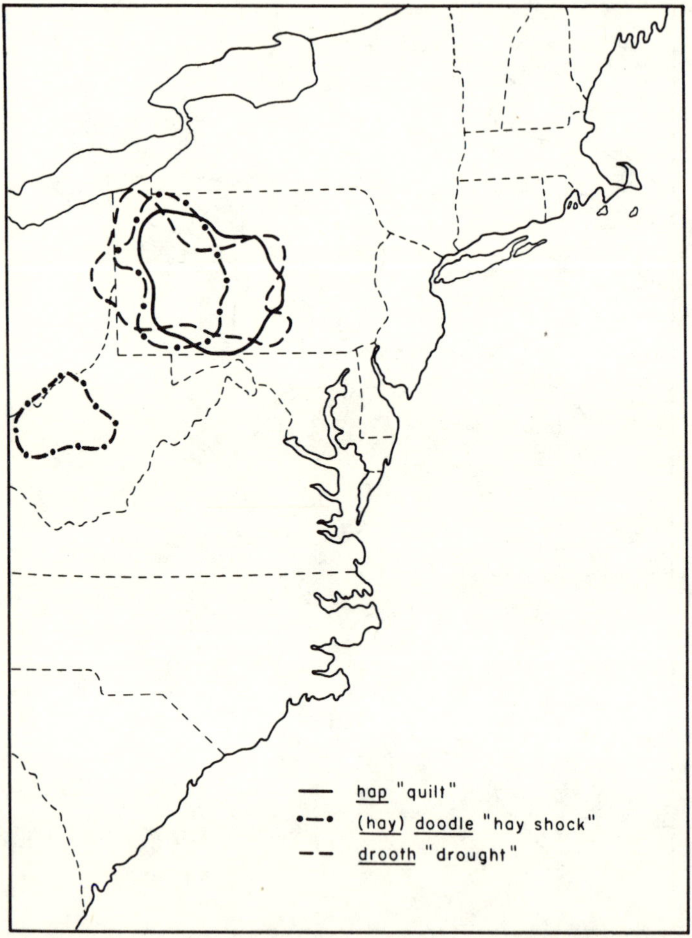


Reprinted from *A Word Geography of the Eastern United States* by Hans Kurath.

# MAP NO. 8

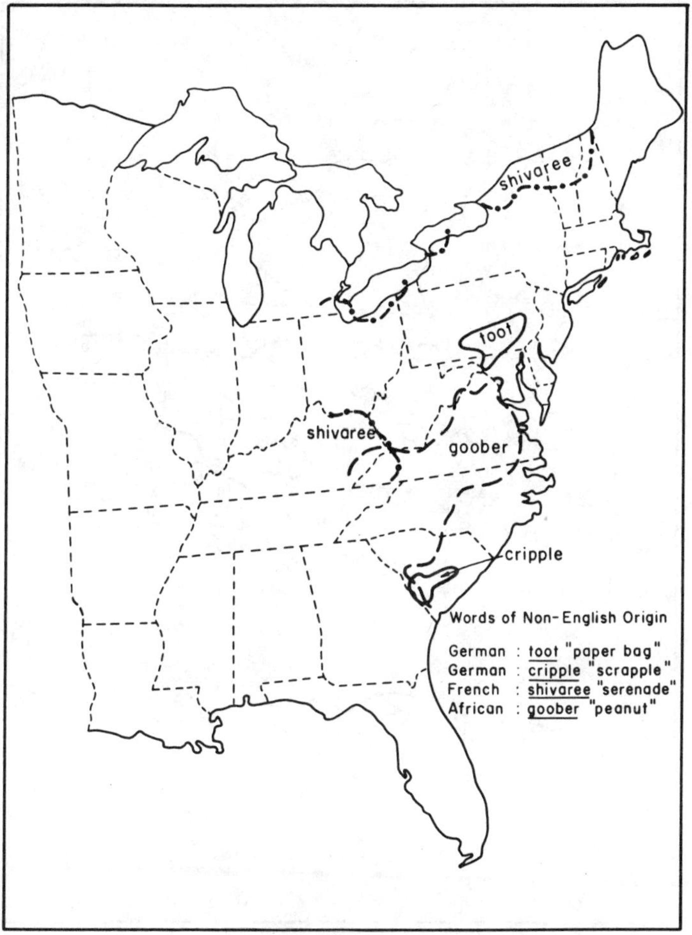


Adapted from a map prepared by Mrs. Raven I. McDavid, Jr., for *The Structure of American English* by W. Nelson Francis.

## MAP NO. 9

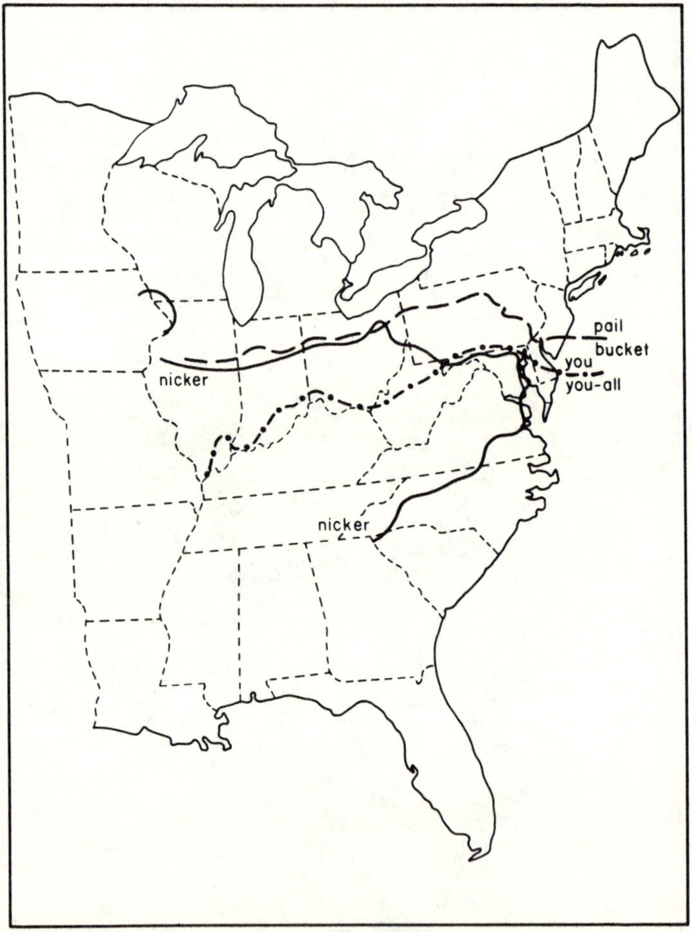


Reprinted from *A Word Geography of the Eastern United States* by Hans Kurath.

# MAP NO. 10

Reprinted from *A Word Geography of the Eastern United States* by Hans Kurath.

# MAP NO. 11

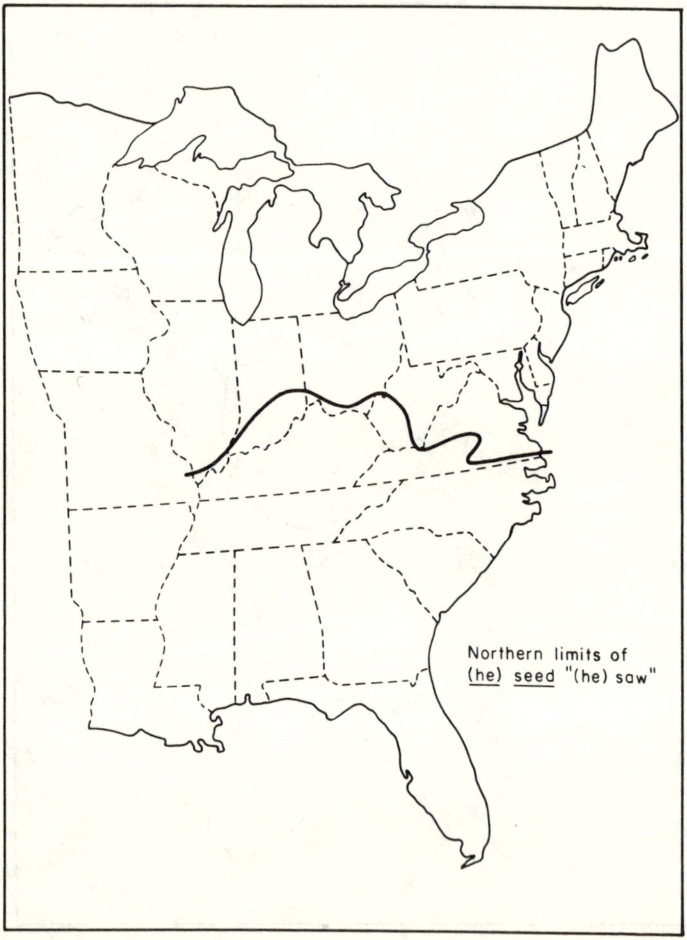


From the files of the Linguistic Atlas of the United States through permission of the editors.

# MAP NO. 12

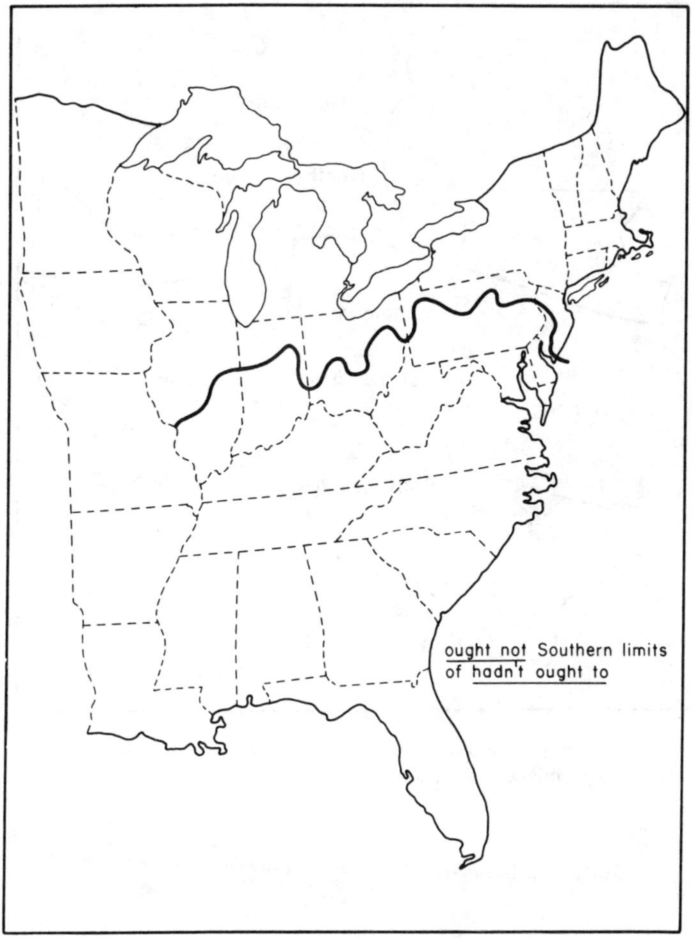


From the files of the Linguistic Atlas of the United States through permission of the editors.

## MAP NO. 13

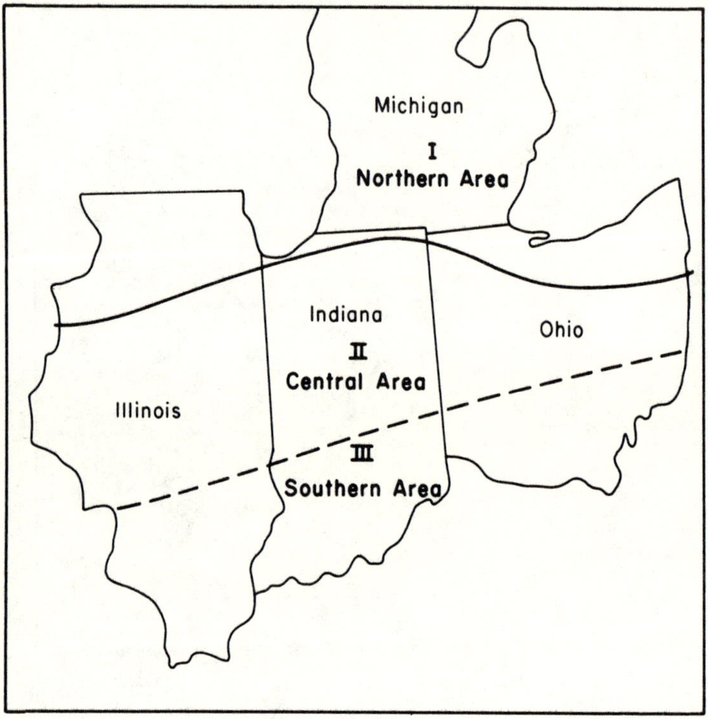


Reproduced from *A Word Atlas of the Great Lakes States* by Alva L. Davis, with permission of the author.

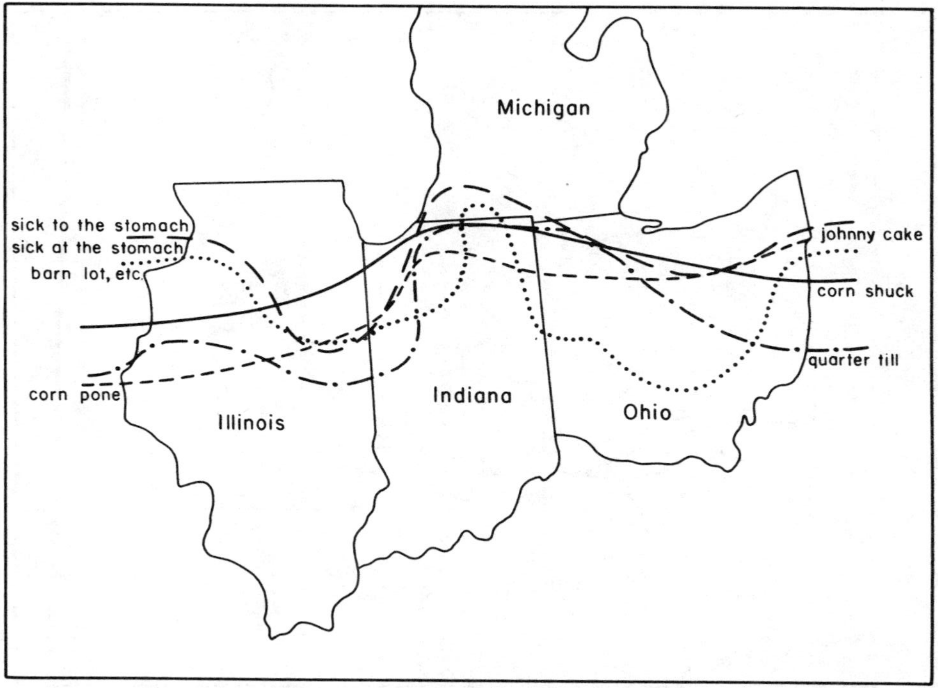


Reproduced from *A Word Atlas of the Great Lakes States* by Alva L. Davis, with permission of the author.

## MAP NO. 15

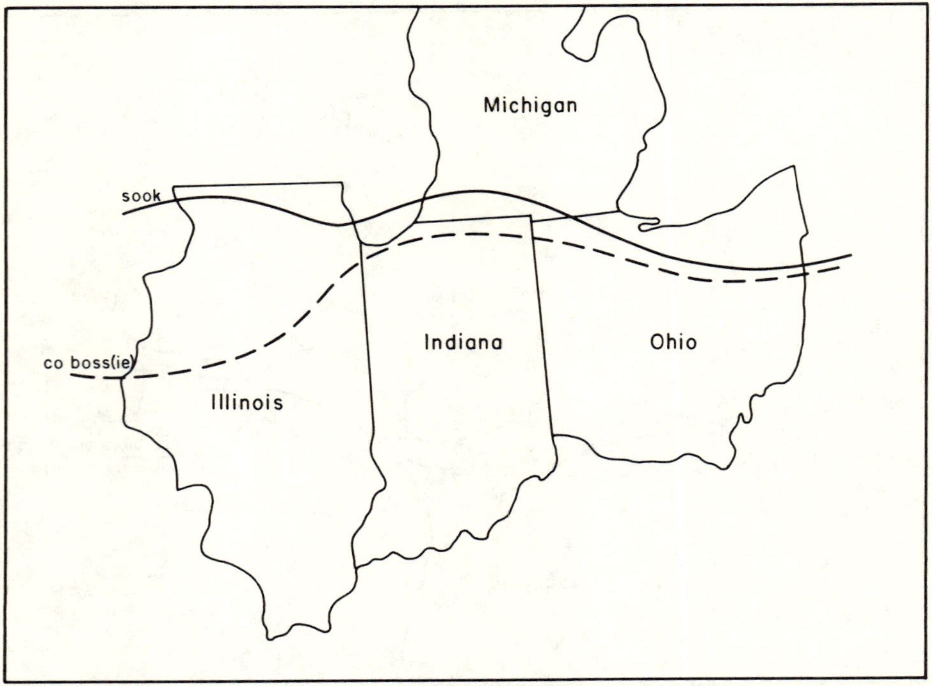


Reproduced from *A Word Atlas of the Great Lakes States* by Alva L. Davis, with permission of the author.

## MAP NO. 16

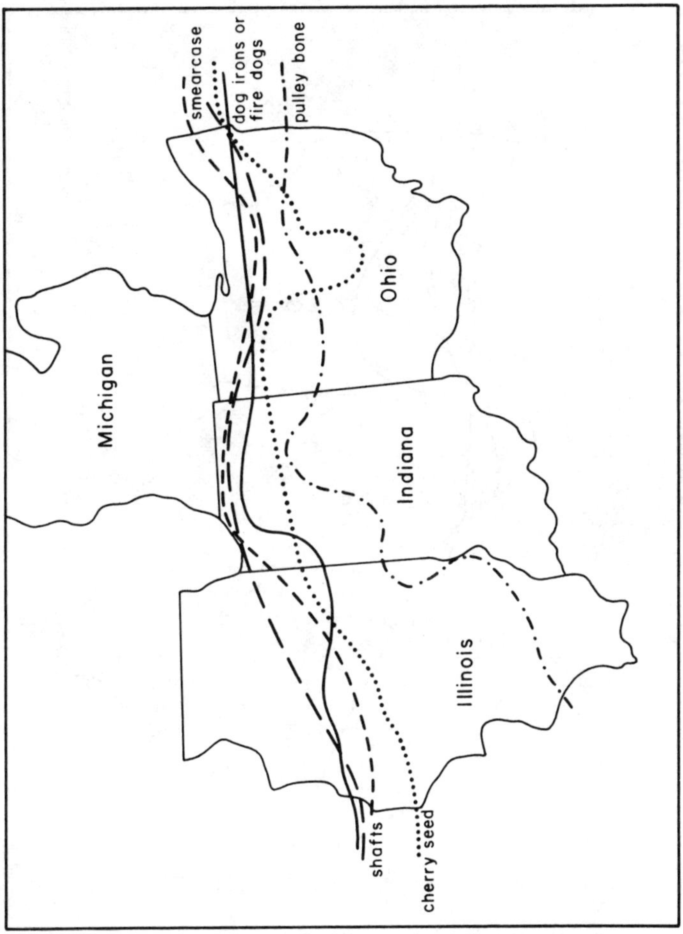


Reproduced from *A Word Atlas of the Great Lakes States* by Alva L. Davis, with permission of the author.

## MAP NO. 17

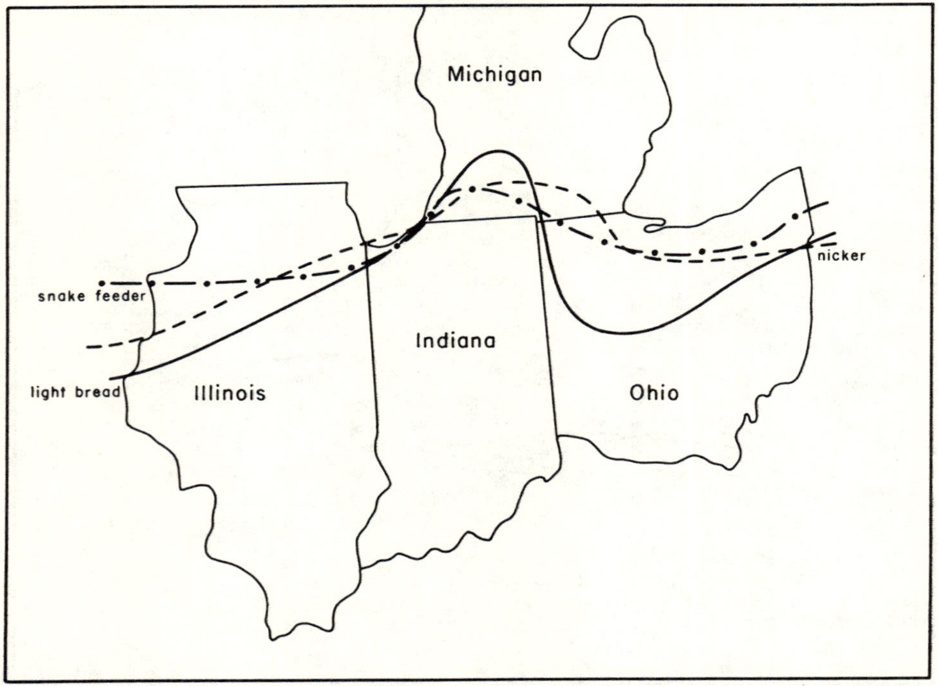


Reproduced from *A Word Atlas of the Great Lakes States* by Alva L. Davis, with permission of the author.

# MAP NO. 18

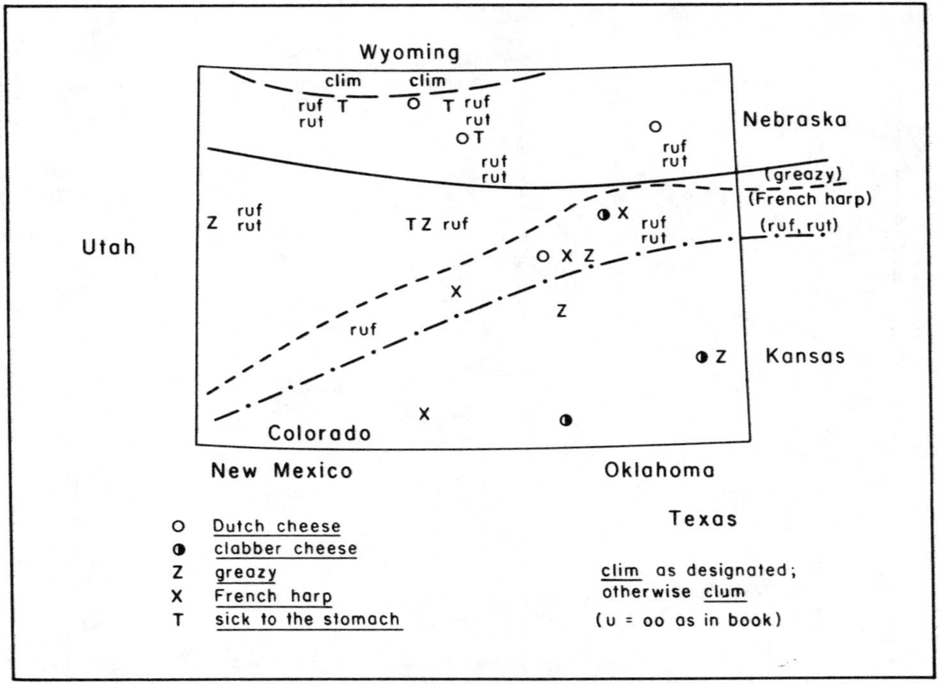


Adapted and reprinted from "Problems of Linguistic Geography in the Rocky Mountain Area," by Kimmerle, McDavid, and McDavid.

# MAP NO. 19

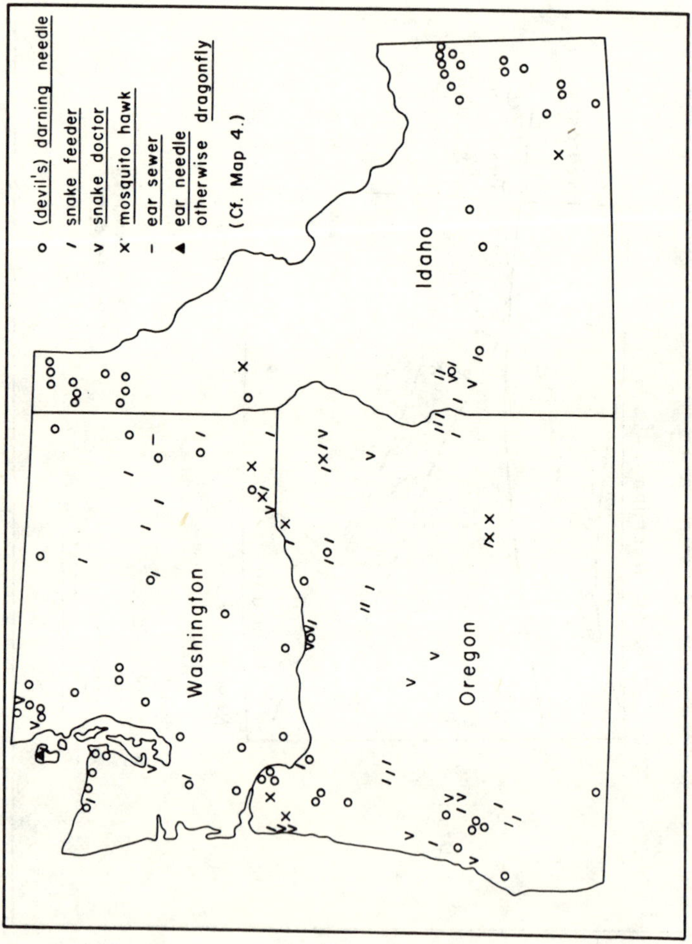
o (devil's) darning needle
/ snake feeder
v snake doctor
x mosquito hawk
– ear sewer
▲ ear needle
otherwise dragonfly
(Cf. Map 4.)
Washington
Oregon
Idaho

MAP NO. 20

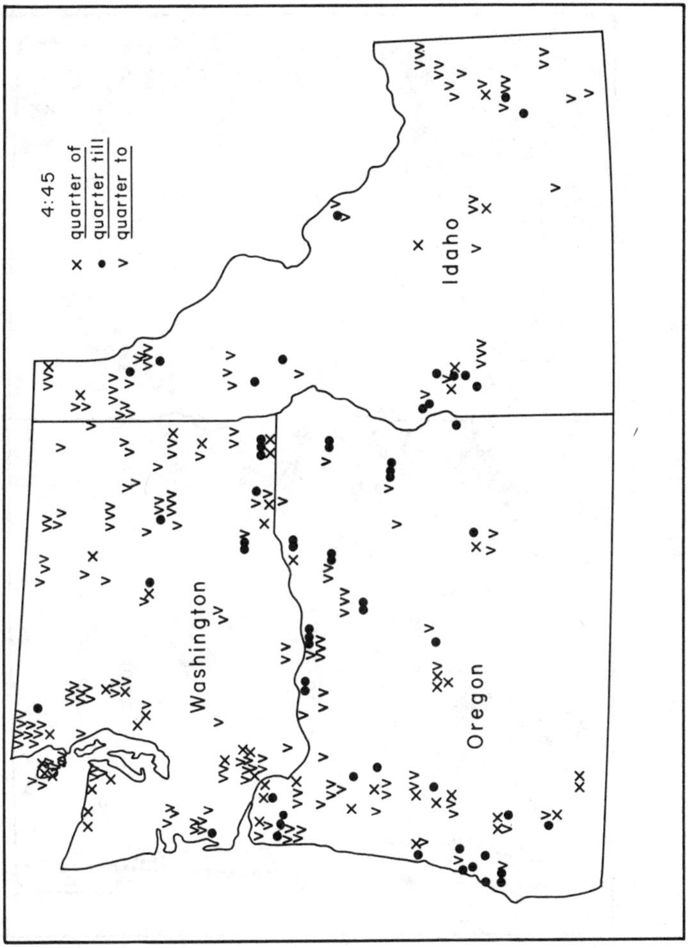
4:45
x quarter of
• quarter till
v quarter to
Washington
Oregon
Idaho

MAP NO. 21

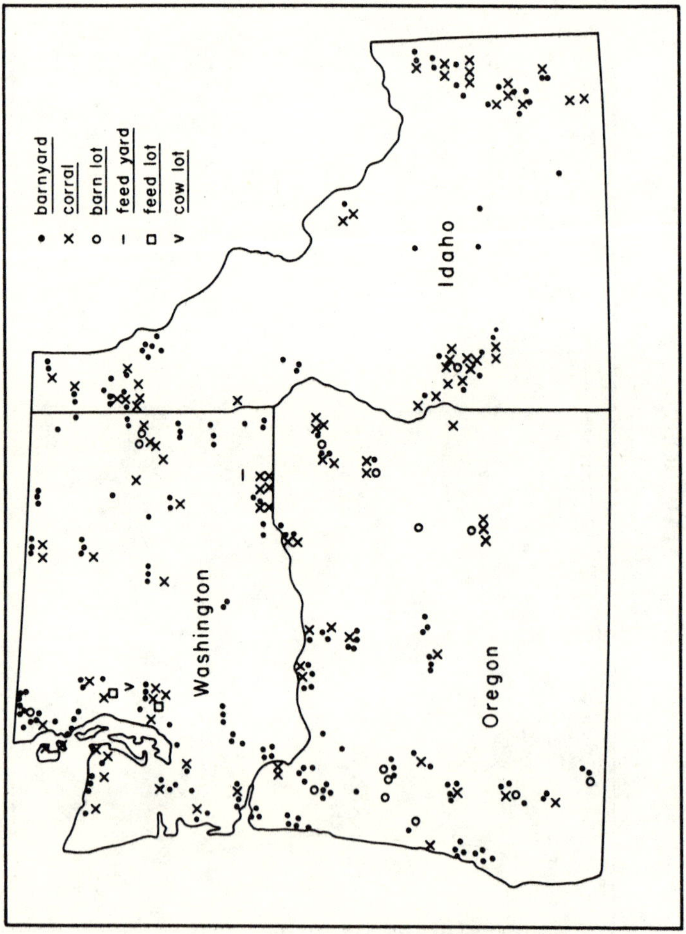
• barnyard
x corral
o barn lot
– feed yard
□ feed lot
v cow lot
Washington
Oregon
Idaho

MAP NO. 22

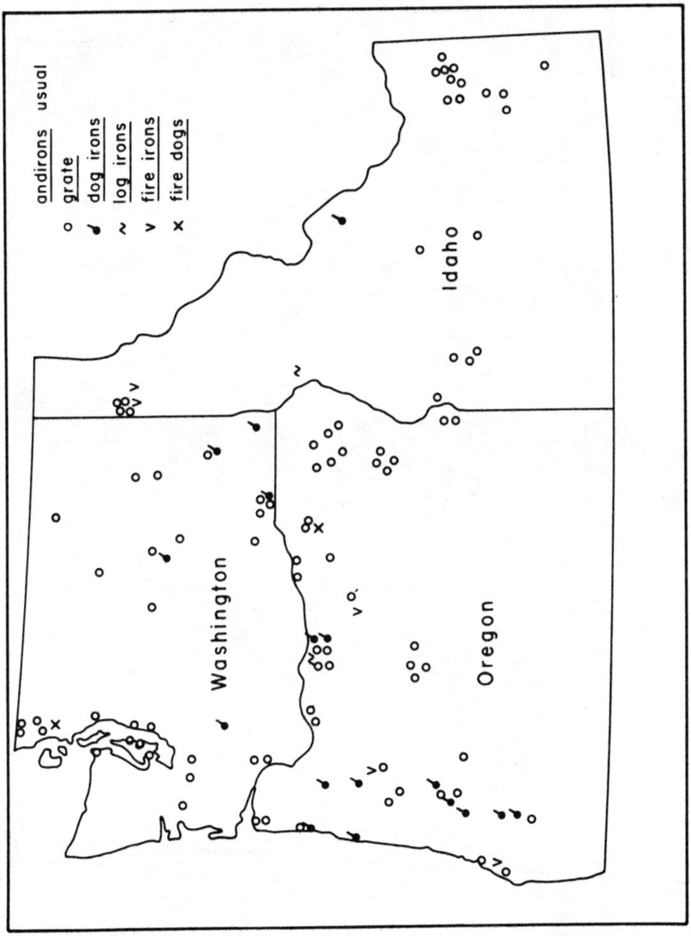
andirons usual
grate
dog irons
log irons
fire irons
fire dogs
Washington
Oregon
Idaho

MAP NO. 23

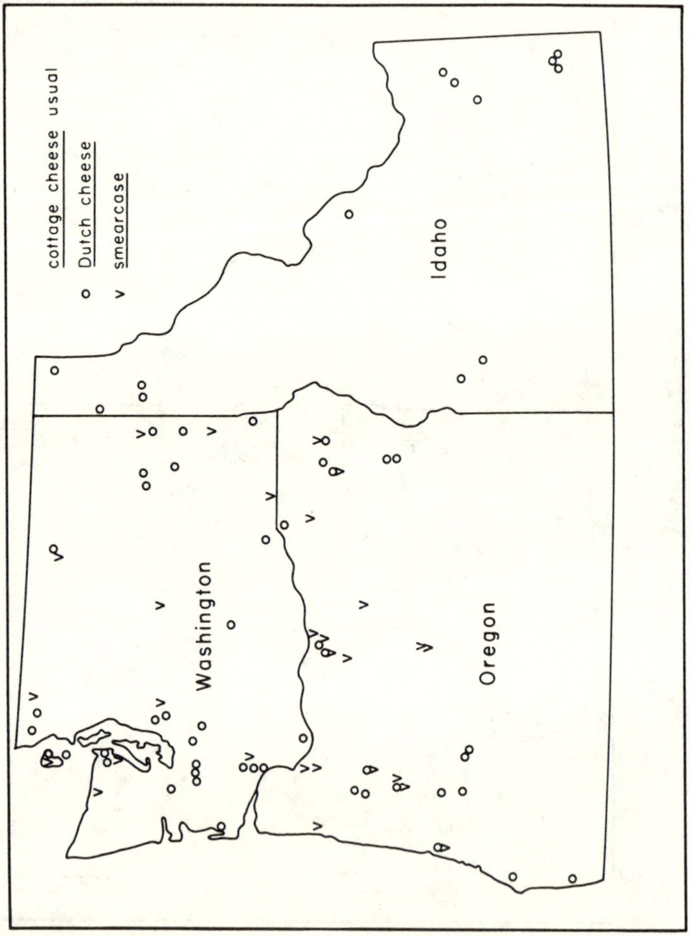
cottage cheese usual
o Dutch cheese
v smearcase
Washington
Oregon
Idaho

MAP NO. 24

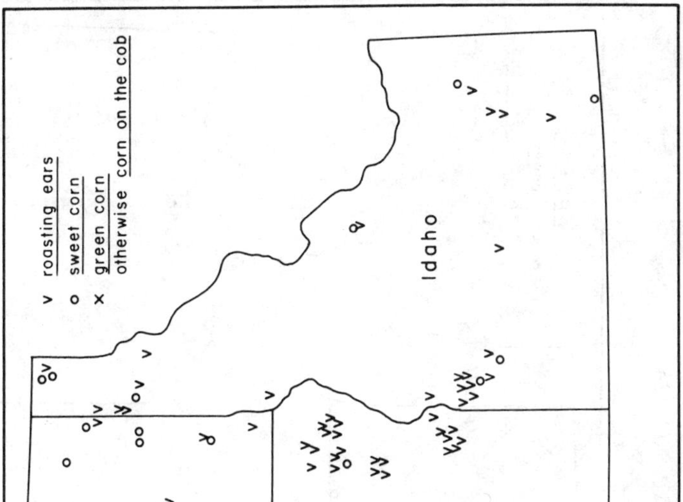
v roasting ears
o sweet corn
x green corn
otherwise corn on the cob
Washington
Oregon
Idaho

MAP NO. 25

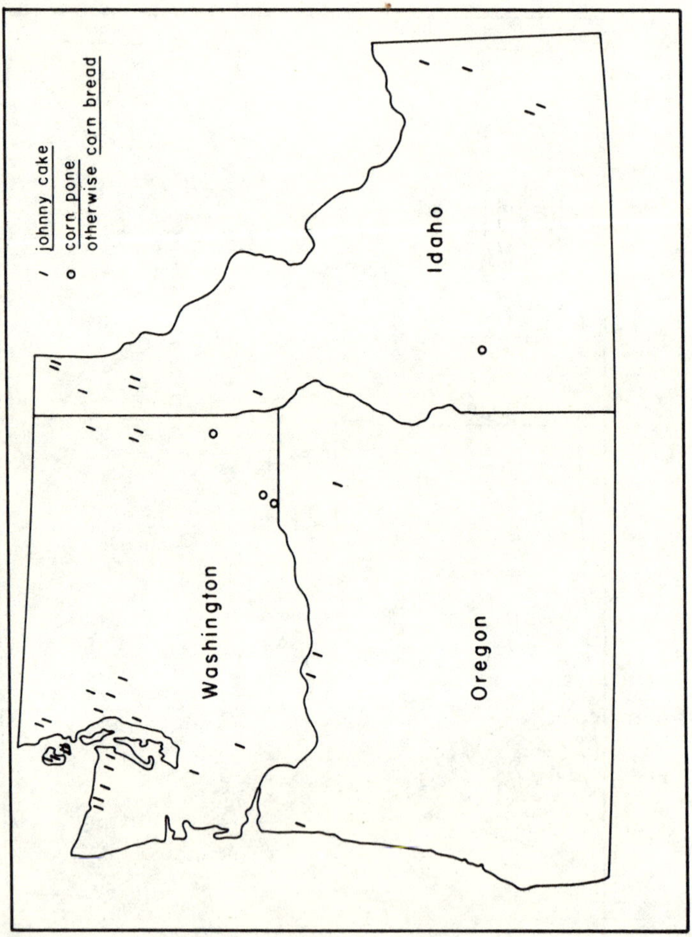
/ johnny cake
o corn pone
otherwise corn bread
Washington
Idaho
Oregon

MAP NO. 26

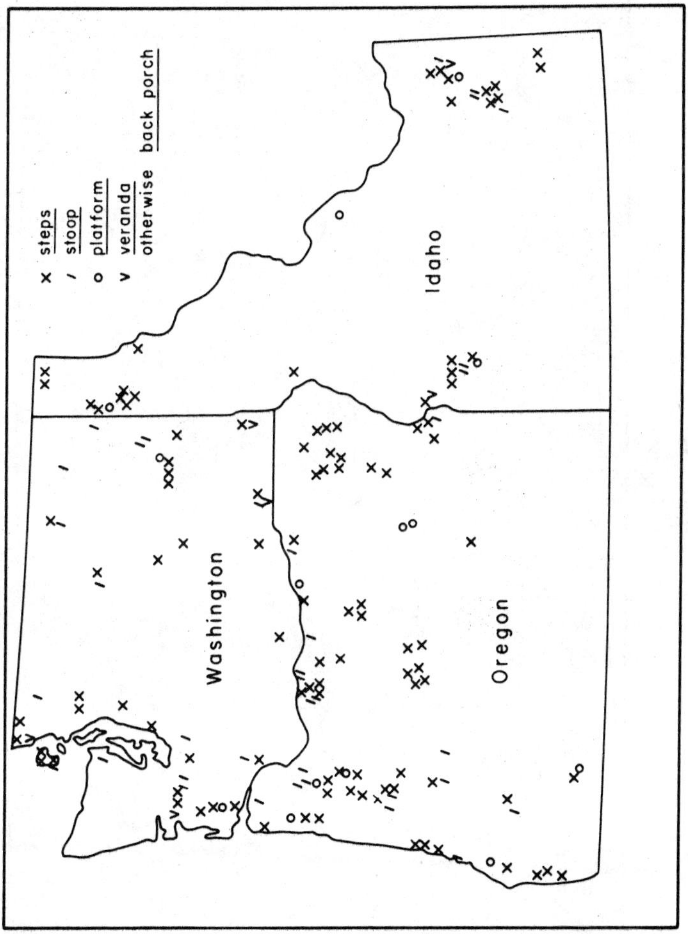
x steps
/ stoop
o platform
v veranda
otherwise back porch
Washington
Oregon
Idaho

MAP NO. 27

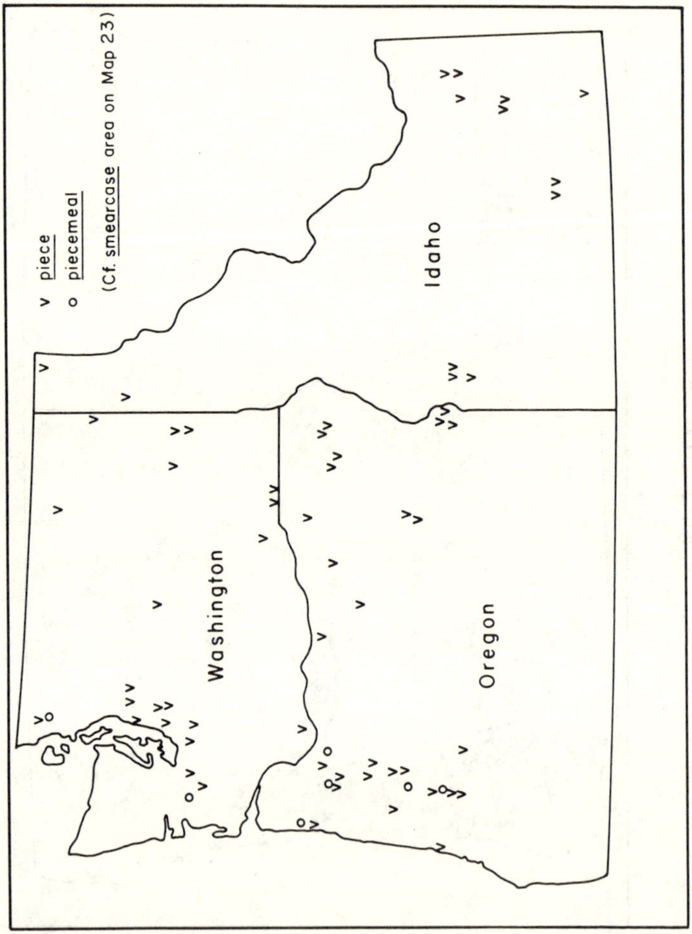
v piece
o piecemeal
(Cf. smearcase area on Map 23)
Washington
Idaho
Oregon

MAP NO. 28

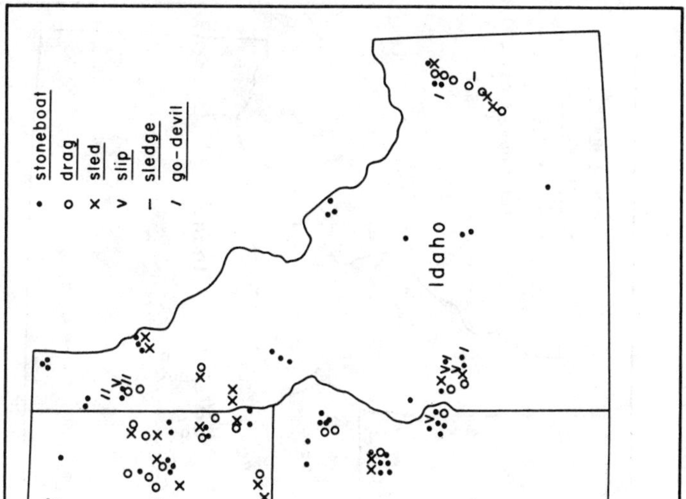
• stoneboat
o drag
x sled
v slip
– sledge
/ go-devil
Washington
Idaho
Oregon

MAP NO. 29

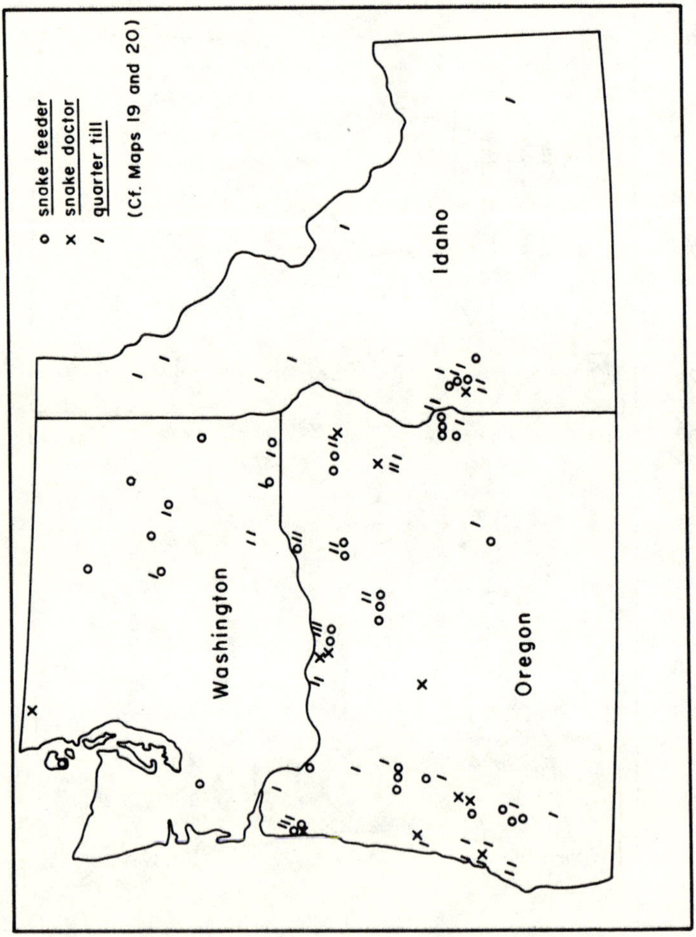
o snake feeder
x snake doctor
/ quarter till
(Cf. Maps 19 and 20)
Idaho
Washington
Oregon

MAP NO. 30

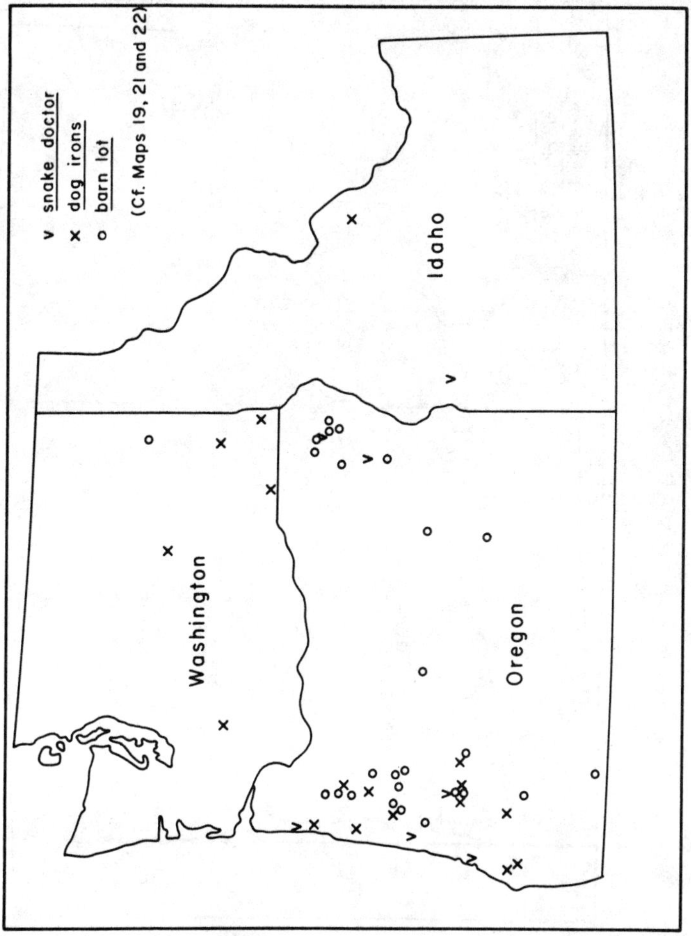
v snake doctor
x dog irons
o barn lot
(Cf. Maps 19, 21 and 22)
Washington
Oregon
Idaho

MAP NO. 31

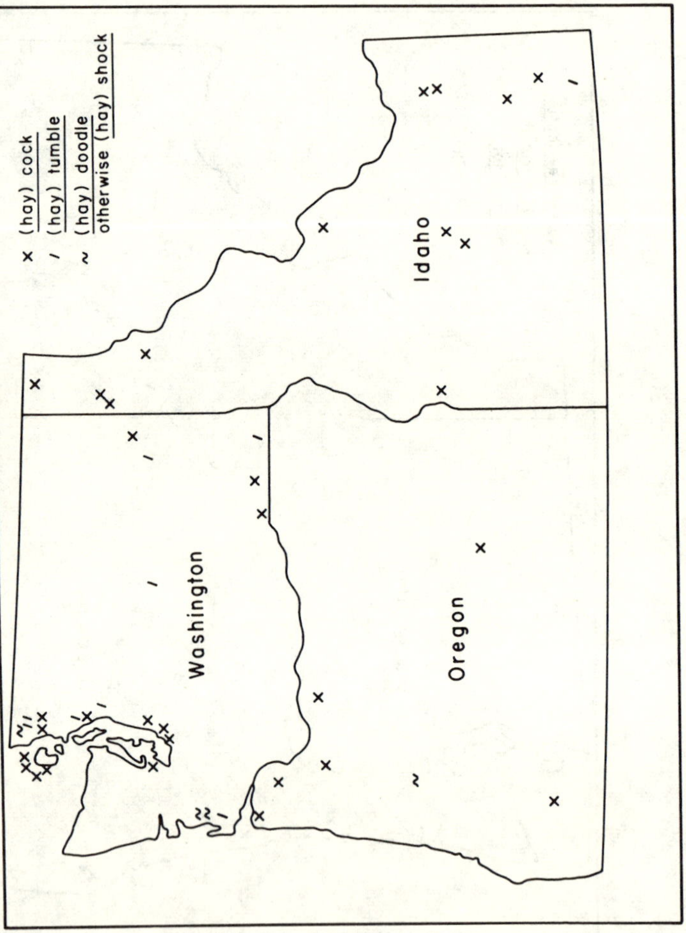
× (hay) cock
/ (hay) tumble
~ (hay) doodle
otherwise (hay) shock
Washington
Oregon
Idaho

MAP NO. 32

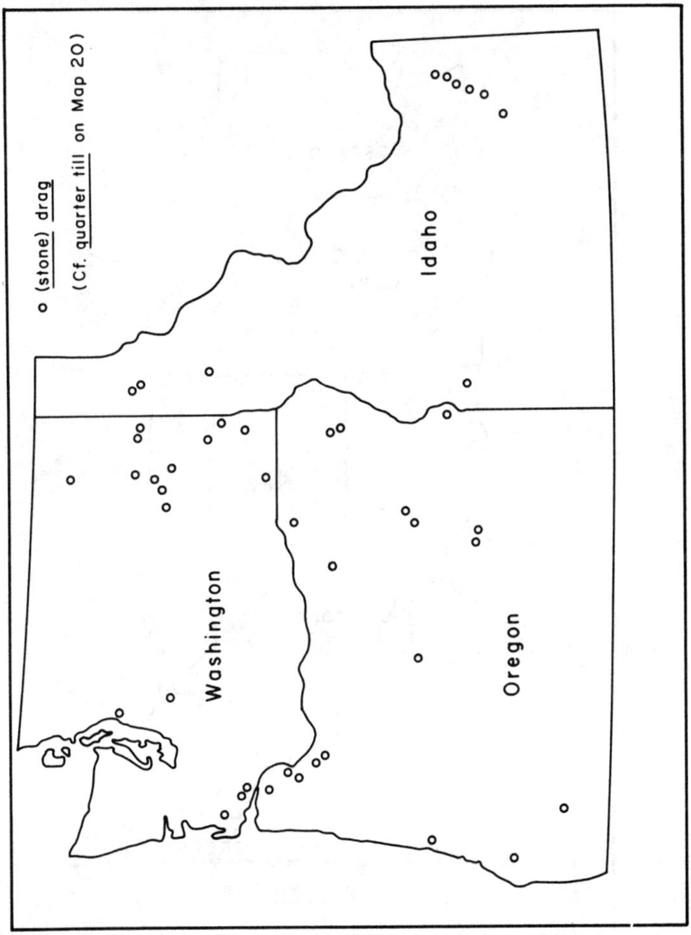
o (stone) drag
(Cf. quarter till on Map 20)
Idaho
Washington
Oregon

Map No. 33

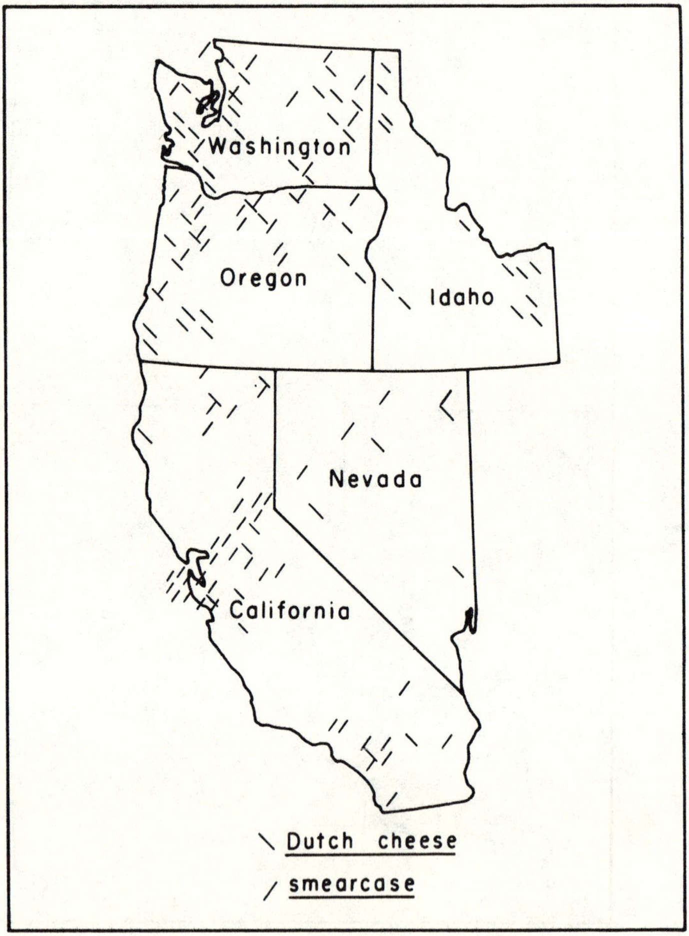
Washington
Oregon
Idaho
Nevada
California
Dutch cheese
smearcase

Map No. 34

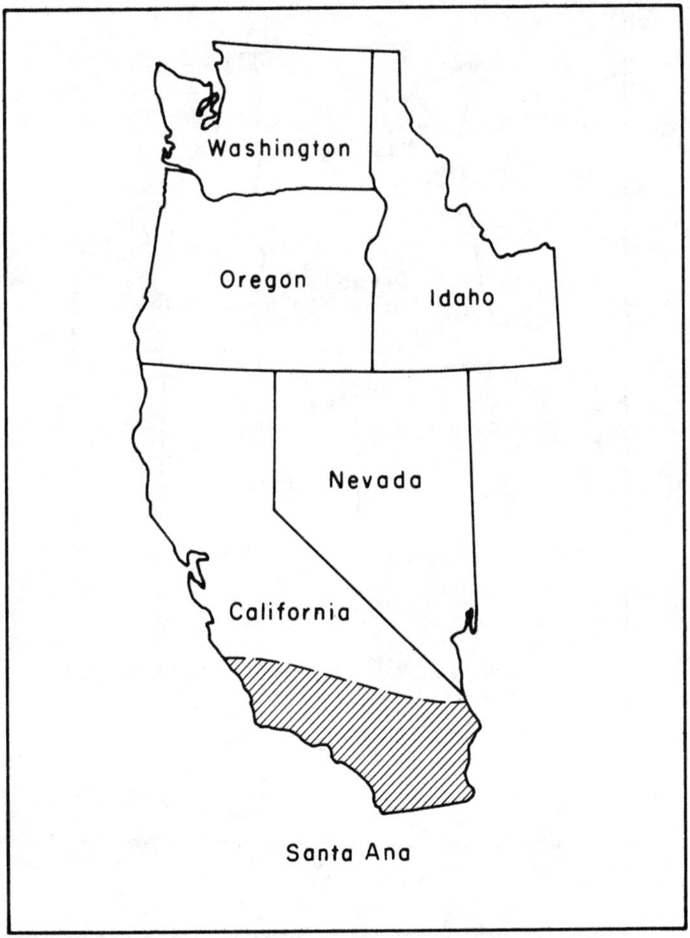

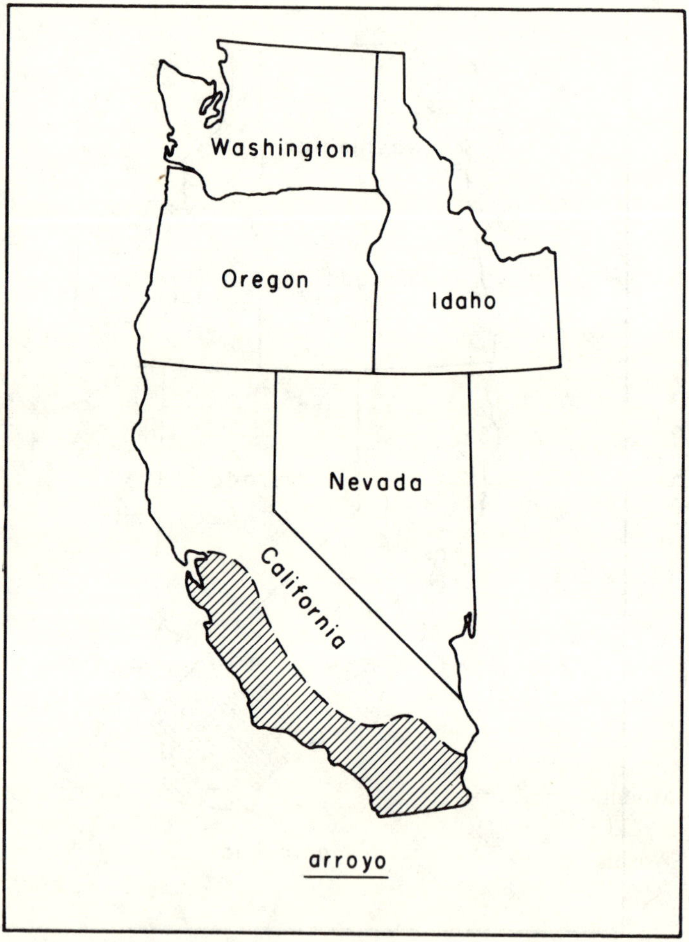


Map No. 35

# *Notes on Maps*

19. *Darning needle* (Northern) occurs chiefly in Washington and Idaho; *snake feeder* (western Midland) is heard mainly in Oregon, plus Columbia River (Palouse) Country of Washington; *snake doctor* (Virginia piedmont) is more restricted; *mosquito hawk* (Southern coastal) is heard occasionally on the Columbia and Snake Rivers.

20. *Quarter of* and *quarter to* are about equally distributed in the Pacific Northwest; *quarter till* (western Midland) corresponds to *snake feeder* in distribution, but is more extended.

21. *Barnyard* (north of the Potomac River, in most of the Ohio Valley) is the usual form in the Northwest, but it competes with the Western *corral; barn lot,* etc. occurs mainly in Oregon, occasionally also around Puget Sound; *corral* is especially dominant in the dry, grassy areas east of the Cascade Mountains.

22. *Andirons* is used everywhere in the Northwest, mostly in Washington; the Western word *grate* is widespread for a referent that is less clearly defined; *dog irons, fire dogs* (South Midland and Southern) are mostly confined to Oregon; *log irons* is possibly a folk etymology, based on *dog irons.*

23. Professor Kurath says: "*Cottage cheese* is a trade name for curds in all eastern states; it is especially common in urbanized areas." The same applies to the Northwest; *Dutch cheese* (Northern, but frequent in the western Midland area) is common in Washington and Idaho, but also frequent in Oregon; *smearcase* (Midland) is heard frequently in Oregon, and its distribution corresponds to that for *snake feeder* (map 19).

24. *Corn on the cob* is common in the Northwest, particularly in Washington; *roasting ears* (Midland and Southern) is more common in Oregon and is quite frequent in Idaho, corresponding in distribution to *quarter till* and *snake feeder; sweet corn* is semantically differentiated as "white corn"; *green corn* appears only at the entrance to Puget Sound and is undoubtedly an older relic of Eastern coastal areas.

25. *Johnny cake* (Northern) is notable here by its demonstration of Northern settlement; *corn pone* (Midland and Southern) occurs only rarely in the Northwest, a fact which is so far unaccountable.

26. *Back porch* is general everywhere; a common variety of architecture is reflected in the expression *steps,* but this is most frequent in Oregon and Idaho, corresponding to the distribution of *roasting ears; stoop* (Northern) occurs with nearly equal frequency in all three states.

27. *Piece(meal)*, like the verb form *piecing,* is of Pennsylvania German origin (thus North Midland); it is more common in the Northwest than *smearcase,* which is also from Pennsylvania German.

28. *Stoneboat* is common throughout the Northwest, particularly in Washington and Idaho; in the East it is described by Kurath as Northern with westward expansion; *stone drag* is a New England form with unexpectedly high frequency in the eastern part of our area; *sled* (Midland and Southern) has also a very high frequency in the Northwest; *go-devil* is especially common in Idaho; *slip* is also peculiar to the Idaho area, but is rare; even more unusual is the term *sledge.*

29. Given here are two eastern Midland forms, *quarter till* and *snake feeder,* along with the Virginia piedmont (South Midland) *snake doctor.*

30. Another combination of forms, this time of the South Midland: *barn lot, dog irons, snake doctor.*

31. *Hay shock* (South Midland and Southern) has become the most common term everywhere in the Northwest; *hay cock* (Northern and North Midland) is frequent in the "Northern" settlements of Washington and Idaho; *hay tumble* is a relic form from northern New England; *hay doodle* is a relic of western Pennsylvania.

32. Here an unusually wide distribution for a New England term is indicated separately; *stone drag* may be compared in distribution to *quarter till.* The fact that a Northern term agrees with one that is definitely Midland is suspicious enough to indicate that the Pacific Northwest may very well give clues to conditions which have changed in the East during the last seventy-five years or more.

Library of Congress Cataloging in Publication Data

Reed, Carroll E.
Dialects of American English.

Bibliography: p.
1. English language in the United States. 2. English language—Dialects—United States. I. Title.
PE2841.R4 1977 427'.9'73 76–45049
ISBN 0–87023–233–9